C. H. Merriam

The geographic distribution of life in North America with special reference to the Mammalia

C. H. Merriam

The geographic distribution of life in North America with special reference to the Mammalia

ISBN/EAN: 9783741105685

Manufactured in Europe, USA, Canada, Australia, Japa

Cover: Foto ©ninafisch / pixelio.de

Manufactured and distributed by brebook publishing software
(www.brebook.com)

C. H. Merriam

The geographic distribution of life in North America with special reference to the Mammalia

VOL. VII, PP. 1-64   APRIL, 1892

PROCEEDINGS

OF THE

BIOLOGICAL SOCIETY OF WASHINGTON.

\

THE GEOGRAPHIC DISTRIBUTION OF LIFE IN NORTH AMERICA WITH SPECIAL REFERENCE TO THE MAMMALIA.*

BY C. HART MERRIAM, M. D.

CONTENTS.

* Annual Presidential Address, delivered at the Twelfth Anniversary Meeting of the Biological Society of Washington, February 6, 1892.

INTRODUCTORY REMARKS.

Nine years ago the Biological Society listened to an address from its distinguished retiring President, Professor Gill, on "The Principles of Zoogeography," or the science of the geographical distribution of animals.* Professor Gill assembled the oceans of the globe, as well as the land areas, into primary divisions or

---

* Proc. Biological Society of Washington, vol. II, 1884, 1–39.

'zoological realms,' of which he recognized 9 for the land and 5 for the sea. It is not my purpose to discuss the zoological regions of the whole world, but to lay before you some of the facts concerned in the distribution of terrestrial animals and plants in North America with special reference to the number and boundaries of the sub-regions and minor life areas, and to touch upon the causes that have operated in their production.

No phenomenon in the whole realm of nature forced itself earlier upon the notice of man than certain facts of geographic distribution. The daily search for food, the first and principal occupation of savage man, directed his attention to the unequal distribution of animals and plants. He not only noticed that certain kinds were found in rivers, ponds, or the sea, and others on land, and that some terrestrial kinds were never seen except in forests, while others were as exclusively restricted to open prairies, but he observed further, when his excursions were extended to more distant localities or from the valleys and plains to the summits of neighboring mountains, that unfamiliar fruits and insects and birds and mammals were met with, while those he formerly knew disappeared.

Thus primeval man, and in truth the ancestors of primeval man, learned by observation the great fact of geographic distribution, the fact that particular kinds of animals and plants are not uniformly diffused over the earth, but are restricted to more or less circumscribed areas.

It will be observed that two classes of cases are here referred to, namely, (1) cases in which in the same general region certain species are restricted to swamps or lowlands, while others are confined to dense forests or rocky hillsides—differences of *station*, and (2) cases in which, regardless of *local* peculiarities, a general change takes place in the fauna and flora in passing from one region to another, or from low valleys or plains to high mountains—*geographic* differences. The latter class only is here considered.

Every intelligent schoolboy knows that elephants, lions, giraffes and chimpanzees inhabit Africa; that orangs and flying lemurs live in Borneo; kangaroos in Australia; the apteryx in New Zealand; the Royal Bengal tiger in India; llamas, chinchillas and sloths in South America; the yak in the high table lands of Thibet, and so on. In accordance with these facts naturalists long ago began to divide the surface of the globe into zoological and botanical regions irrespective of the long recognized geographic and political divisions.* It was found that different degrees of relationship exist between the indigenous animals and plants of different countries, and that as a rule the more remote and isolated the region and the earlier in geologic time its separation took place, the more distinct were its inhabitants from those of other regions. Each of the larger islands lying near the equator and the continental masses of the southern hemisphere were found to possess not only peculiar species and genera, but even families and orders not found elsewhere; and it was discovered that insular areas of considerable magnitude that have had no land connection with other areas since very early times possess faunas and floras remarkable for the antiquity of their dominant types. In Australia, the most disconnected of all the continents, the entire mammalian fauna, though wonderfully diversified in appearance and habits, belongs to the primitive orders of monotremes and marsupials, whose best known representatives are the duck-billed platypus and the kangaroo. In the latter group Australia and neighboring islands contain no less than six families not found in any other part of the world.

Madagascar is the exclusive home of the remarkable aye-aye (*Chiromys*) and *Cryptoprocta*, the latter believed to be intermediate between the cats and civets.

Tropical America is alone in the possession of true ant-eaters (*Myrmecophagidæ*), sloths (*Bradypodidæ*), marmosets (*Hapalidæ*), armadillos (*Dasypodidæ*) and agouties (*Dasyproctidæ*).

Africa is the home of many groups not known elsewhere. Among them are the giraffe, hippopotamus, *Orycteropus*, elephant shrews (*Macroscelididæ*), *Potomogale*, and *Chrysochloridæ*.

Besides this class of cases, in which particular groups are restricted to particular countries, there is another class, in which the living representatives of single groups exist in isolated colonies in widely separated parts of the world. Illustrations of this kind are furnished by the tapirs, which inhabit tropical America and the Malay Peninsula, but do not exist in intermediate lands; by the family *Camelidæ*, represented in South America by the llamas and in parts of Eurasia by the true camels; and by a group

---

*Among the many distinguished naturalists who have contributed to the literature of the subject may be mentioned Humboldt, Bonpland, Buffon, De Candolle, Schouw, Engler, Agassiz, Baird, Asa Gray, Grisebach, Huxley, Gill, Allen, Wallace, and Packard.

of insectivorous mammals in which all the genera but one are restricted to Madagascar, the one exception (*Solenodon*) living in Cuba and Haiti. Examples of this sort are known as cases of *discontinuous* distribution, and indicate that the ancestors of the animals in question formerly inhabited a vast extent of country ; that some sort of land connection, however indirect, existed between the colonies now so widely separated, and that the surviving descendants of these groups are probably approaching extinction.

The examples thus far cited relate to the disconnected land areas in the neighborhood of the equator or in the southern hemisphere, and their explanation is to be sought in the history of the past. In the northern hemisphere animals and plants in general have a much more extended distribution than in the southern, the majority of the larger groups being common to North America, Europe, and Asia, and the limits of their distribution are encountered in traveling in a north and south direction and are evidently the result of causes now in operation. It is to this class of cases as presented on the North American continent that your attention is invited this evening.

In passing from the tropics to the Arctic pole on the eastern side of America a number of distinct zones are crossed, the most conspicuous features of which are well known. In the plant world the palms, mangroves, mahogany, mastic, Jamaica dogwood, and cassias of the tropical coast districts are succeeded by the magnolias, pawpaws, sweet-gums, hackberries, and persimmons of the Southern States. These give place gradually to the oaks, chestnuts, and hickories of the Middle States; and the latter to the groves of aspen, maple, and beech which reach the southern edge of the great coniferous forest of the north—a forest of spruces and firs that stretches completely across the continent from Labrador to Alaska. Beyond this forest is a treeless expanse whose distant shores are bathed in the icy waters of the Arctic Ocean.

Concurrently with these changes in vegetation from the south northward occur equally marked differences in the mammals, birds, reptiles, and insects. Among mammals the tapirs, monkeys, armadillos, nasuas, peccaries, and opossums of Central America and Mexico are replaced to the northward by woodrats, marmots, chipmunks, foxes, rabbits, short-tailed field-mice of several genera, shrews, wild-cats, lynxes, short-tailed porcupines, elk, moose, reindeer, sables, fishers, wolverines, lemmings, musk oxen, and polar bears.

The trogons, saw-bills, parrots, cotingas and other birds of tropical America give place in turn to the cardinals, blue grosbeaks, mocking birds, tufted tits, and gnatcatchers of the Southern States; the chewink, indigo bird, tanager, bluebird, and robin of the Middle and Northern States; the Canada jays, crossbills, white-throated sparrows, and hawk owls of the northern coniferous forests, and the ptarmigans, snowy owls, and snowflakes of the Arctic circle.

Historical Synopsis of Faunal and Floral Divisions Proposed for North America.

The recognition of the above-mentioned facts early led to attempts to divide the surface of the land into faunal and floral regions or zones, and no less than 56 authors have proposed such divisions for North America. Of these, 31 were zoologists and 25 botanists. Of the zoologists, 10 aimed to show the distribution of animals in general, 8 of birds, 4 of terrestrial mollusks, 3 of mammals, 1 of reptiles and batrachians, and 4 of insects. Of the botanists, 22 aimed to show the distribution of plants in general and 3 of forest trees.

Of the writers who attempted to indicate the life areas of the New World prior to 1850, 68 percent were botanists, while during the next twenty years (1850–1870), 65 percent were zoologists. This striking oscillation of the biologic pendulum, first toward botany and then toward zoology, may be attributed in part at least to the influence of two great minds—Humboldt and Agassiz. Humboldt laid the corner-stone of the philosophic study of plant geography in 1805. Stimulated by his example and writings, botanists led the way and were almost the only occupants of the field until the middle of the present century, when the influence of the elder Agassiz gained the ascendency and the botanists were replaced by zoologists, who have been in the lead ever since.

The accompanying table shows the various authors referred to, the dates of the earliest publication of their divisions, the branch of biology on which their conclusions were based, and states whether or not their articles were accompanied by maps.

Latreille	1817	Insects	No map
De Candolle (Aug.)	1820	Plants	No map
Schouw	1822	Plants	Map
Martius	1824–'26	Plants	Map
Minding	1829	Mammals	No map
Pickering	1830	Plants	Map
Lesson	1831	Birds	No map
De Candolle (Alph.)	1835	Plants	No map
Meyen	1836	Plants	No map
Pompper	1841	Animals	No map
Berghaus	1833	Plants	Map
Martens and Galeotti	1842	Plants	No map
Hinds	1843	Plants	No map
Frankenheim	1843	Plants	No map
Wagner	1844	Mammals	Map
Richard and Galeotti	1844	Plants	No map
Binney (A.)	1851	Mollusks	No map
Richardson	1851	Plants	No map
Schmarda	1853	Animals	Map
Agassiz	1854	Animals	Map
Gray	1856	Plants	No map
Woodward	1856	Mollusks	Map
Sclater	1858	Birds	No map
Le Conte	1859	Insects	Map
Cooper	1859	Forests	Map
Hooker	1861	Plants	Map
Binney (W. G.)	1863	Mollusks	Map
Verrill	1863	Birds	No map
Baird	1866	Birds	No map
Murray	1866	Mammals	Map
Grisebach	1866	Plants	Map
Huxley	1868	Animals	Map
Brown	1870	Forests	Map
Allen	1871	Animals	No map
Blyth	1871	Animals	No map
Cope	1873	Repts. and batrchs.	Map
Porter	1874	Plants	Map
Scudder	1874	Insects	Map
Wallace	1876	Animals	Map
Dyer	1878	Plants	No map
Engler	1882	Plants	Map
Packard	1883	Animals	Map
Jordan	1883	Mollusks	Map
Sargent	1884	Forests	Map
Drude	1884	Plants	Map
Hartlaub	1886	Birds	Map
Reichenow	1887	Birds	Map
Heilprin	1887	Animals	Map

Hemsley............ 1887............... Plants............ Map
Brendel............. 1887............... Plants............ No map
Nelson.............. 1887............... Birds .... No map
Schwarz .... 1888............... Insects .... No map
Bessey.............. 1888............... Plants............ No map
Ridgway........... 1889............... Birds .... No map
Merriam .... 1890............... Animals and plants. Map
Keeler.............. 1891............... Birds............. Map

The principal bio-geographic divisions that have been recognized by a large number of writers, and as a rule have been proposed independently and under different names, resulting from the study of different groups, are described in the following synopses, each of which may be regarded as a chronologic synonymy of the region to which it refers.

Arctic Division (Above Limit of Trees).

An Arctic circumpolar division north of the limit of tree growth was recognized as a distinct region by European writers long before the earliest attempts were made to map the faunal and floral areas of North America.* Hence the following table is necessarily incomplete, since it shows only the extent to which this zone has been recognized by those who have actually defined faunal and floral areas in North America.

Date	Author	Name given to region	Study based on	Rank
1820	De Candolle...	Hyperboreal Region....	Plants.............	1
1822	Schouw	Realm of Mosses and Saxifrages.	Plants.............	1
1830	Pickering.....	Arctic Region..........	Plants.............	1
1831	Lesson	Arctic Region..........	Birds	1
1835	De Candolle...	Arctic Region..........	Plants.............	1
1836	Meyen	Polar Zone............	Plants.............	1
1838	Berghaus	Realm of Mosses and Saxifrages.	Plants.............	1
1843	Hinds........	Greenland Region......	Plants.............	1
1844	Wagner	Polar Province........	Mammals	2

* This region, however, is not universally recognized. Wallace and a few others refuse to accept it. Agassiz, Allen, and most botanical writers, on the other hand, regard it as one of the best defined of the primary divisions. An important recent treatise on the subject, from the standpoint of the distribution of mammals, is the following : "*Die arktische Subregion—Ein Beitrag zur geographischen Verbreitung der Thiere,*" by Dr. August Brauer (Zoologische Jahrbucher, Abth. fur. Syst. III, Jan., 1888, 189-308, taf. VIII).

Date	Author	Name given to region	Study based on	Rank
1853	Schmarda	Barren Grounds........	Animals..........	2
1854	Agassiz.......	Arctic Realm	Animals..........	1
1856	Woodward ...	Region of Saxifrages and Mosses.	Mollusks..........	1
1858	Cooper........	Arctic Province........	Plants.............	1
1866	Grisebach	Arctic-Alpine Region...	Plants.............	1
1870	Brown ....:..	Treeless or Eskimo Province.	Forests............	1
1871	Allen	Arctic Realm...........	Animals..........	1
1875	Cope.........	Arctic Realm...........	Animals..........	1
1878	Dyer........	Arctic-Alpine Flora	Plants.............	2
1882	Engler .\....	Arctic Region..........	Plants..............	2
1883	Packard......	Arctic Realm...........	Animals..........	1
1883	Jordan	Arctic Province........	Mollusks	2
1884	Drude........	Arctic District	Plants.............	2
1887	Brendel.......	Arctic-Alpine Division..	Plants.............	1
1887	Reichenow....	Arctic Zone............	Birds....:........	1
1887	Nelson	Arctic District (Alaskan).	Birds.............	1
1888	Brauer	Arctic Subregion.......	Mammals	2
1890	Merriam......	Arctic Region..........	Animals and plants.	2

Boreal Division.

This heading is intended to cover the zone of coniferous forests extending across the continent south of the *Arctic Realm.* While its northern boundary is fixed at the limit of trees, its southern border has been variously placed by different writers. Schouw did not recognize it at all, but carried his great forest region down to latitude 36°, where the true southern district begins. Berghaus, who in other respects followed Schouw, divided this great region into two parts, the northernmost of which he named the 'Realm of Conifers,' placing its southern limit in the east at about latitude 47°. Hinds, Agassiz, Woodward, Verrill, and Drude speak of it as the 'Canadian' Region. Its southern limit is here extended to include the 'Canadian Fauna' of recent zoological writers.

The extent to which this zone has been recognized will appear from the following table:

Date	Author	Name given to region	Study based on	Rank
1830	Pickering	Canadian Flora........	Plants.............	2
1838	Berghaus	Realm of Conifers......	Plants.............	1
1843	Hinds........	Canadian Region.......	Plants.............	1
1853	Schmarda	Region of Coniferous Forests.	Animals..........	2

Date	Author	Name given to region	Study based on	Rank
1854	Agassiz.......	Canadian Fauna.......	Animals...........	2
1856	Woodward ...	Canadian Province.....	Mollusks..........	1
1856	Gray.........	Middle and Northern Wooded District.	Plants.............	(?)
1859	Le Conte.....	Northern Province.....	Insects............	2
1859	Cooper	Lacustrian Province....	Forests............	1
1863	Verrill	Canadian Fauna.......	Birds.............	1
1863	Binney.......	Northern Region.......	Mollusks	2
1870	Brown	Lacustrian Province....	Forests............	1
1871	Allen	Hudsonian and Canadian Faunas.	Animals...........	3
1882	Engler	Region of Conifers.....	Plants.............	2
1883	Packard......	Boreal Province........	Animals...........	1
1884	Sargent.......	Northern Forest........	Forests............	2
1884	Drude........	Canadian District......	Plants.............	2
1890	Merriam	Boreal Region.........	Animals and plants.	2

Atlantic, Central, and Pacific Divisions of Temperate North America.

It has been the custom of recent writers to divide the broad middle zone of North America (most of which lies within the United States) into three main divisions—*Atlantic* or *Eastern*, stretching from the Atlantic Ocean to the eastern border of the plains; *Central*, from the plains to the Sierra Nevada; and *Pacific*, from the Sierra to the Pacific Ocean.* These regions were proposed as early as 1854 by the elder Agassiz, who however divided the Eastern or Atlantic district into two regions of equal rank—*Alleghanian* and *Louisianian*, or faunas of the Middle and the Southern States. In this respect he has been followed by Cope. Other authors, including Le Conte, Baird, and Allen, regard the southern district as only a subdivision of the Eastern region. Agassiz named the Central region the '*Table-land or Rocky Mountain Fauna*' and the Pacific the '*Californian Fauna.*'

This arrangement of the United States into three provinces has been followed in the main by Le Conte (1859), W. G. Binney (1863), Baird (1866), Cope (1873), Grisebach (1875), Wallace

---

*These divisions must not be confounded with those of Amos Binney (published in 1851) bearing the same names, for Binney's Atlantic region lay between the Atlantic and Alleghanies, his Central region between the Alleghanies and the Rocky mountains, and his Pacific region between the Rocky mountains and the Pacific. Woodward's divisions (1856) are essentially those of Amos Binney.

(1876), Allen (1878), Packard (1883), Jordan (1883), Hartlaub & Newton (1886), and Heilprin (1887).

The three divisions will be considered separately.

Atlantic or Eastern Forest Region.—Many writers have recognized an eastern forest region stretching from the plains to the Atlantic and in a general way from the boreal or coniferous forests of the north to the alluvial lands of the South Atlantic and Gulf States; but its northern and southern limits have been by no means agreed upon. Schouw defined these boundaries as the limit of trees on the north and latitude 36° on the south, and named the region Michaux's Realm or *Realm of Asters and Solidagos.* Berghaus retained Schouw's southern boundary, but took off a broad belt on the north, which he named the *Realm of Coniferous Forests.* The resulting northern limit as shown on his map (1838) agrees closely with that adopted by such recent writers as Wallace (1876), Allen (1878), Packard (1883), and Heilprin (1887), all of whom, on the other hand, carry its southern boundary south to the Gulf of Mexico, thus making it co-extensive with the *Atlantic or Eastern Province* already referred to.

Several early writers, among whom Schouw and Berghaus were prominent, recognized this region in the east, but knew nothing of the great interior plains, and consequently spoke of it as extending all the way to the Rocky mountains.

The extent to which this Eastern Forest region has been recognized, together with the approximate north and south boundaries assigned it, will appear from the following table:

NOTE.—In the columns showing limit on the north and south the following abbreviations are used: L. T. = northern limit of trees; C. F. = northern coniferous forests; A. = Austroriparian or Louisianian region; G. = Gulf of Mexico.

Date	Author	Name given to region	Limit on the North	South	Based on	Rank
1822	Schouw	Asters and Solidagos.	L. T.	A.	Plants ...	1
1830	Pickering	Flora of United States	C. F.	G.	Plants....	2
1838	Berghaus	Asters and Solidagos.	C. F.	A.	Plants ...	1
1843	Hinds	Iroquoian	C. F.	G.	Plants ...	1
1848	Frankenheim	New England	C. F.	A.	Plants ...	2
1854	Agassiz	Alleghanian	C. F.	A.	Animals .	2
1856	Gray	Northern States	(?)	A.	Plants ...	1
1859	Le Conte	Eastern	(?)	G.	Insects...	1
1859	Cooper	Appalachian	C. F.	G.	Forests ..	1

Date	Author	Name given to region	Limit on the North	South	Based on	Rank
1863	Verrill	Alleghanian	C. F.	A.	Birds	1
1863	Binney (W .G.)	Interior	C. F.	A.	Mollusks.	2
1866	Baird	Eastern	C. F.	G.	Birds	1
1866	Grisebach	Forest	L. T.	G.	Plants	1
1870	Brown	Appalachian	C. F.	G.	Forests	1
1871	Allen	Eastern	C. F.	G.	Animals.	2
1873	Cope	Eastern	(?)	A.	Animals.	2
1874	Porter	Forest	C. F.	G.	Plants	1
1876	Wallace	Alleghanian	C. F.	G.	Animals.	2
1882	Engler	Appalachian Province	C. F.	G.	Plants	3
1883	Packard	Eastern	C. F.	G.	Animals.	1
1883	Jordan	Atlantic Region	C. F.	G.	Mollusks.	3
1884	Sargent	Deciduous Forests	C. F.	A.	Forests	2
1884	Drude	Virginian	C. F.	G.	Plants	2
1886	Hartlaub	Alleghanian	C. F.	G.	Birds	2
1887	Heilprin	Alleghanian	C. F.	G.	Animals.	2
1887	Brendel	Mixed Forest	C. F.	G.	Plants	2
1889	Ridgway	Eastern Province	(?)		G.	Birds	1

Central or Middle Division.—This division extends from the eastern border of the great plains to the Sierra Nevada and Cascade Mountains. It was first proposed by Agassiz in 1854, under the name '*Table-land Fauna or Fauna of the Rocky Mountains.*'

The extent to which it has been recognized will appear from the following table:

Date	Author	Name given to region	Based on	Rank
1854	Agassiz	Table-land Fauna	Animals	3
1859	Le Conte	Central District	Insects	1
1863	Binney (W. G.)	Central Province	Mollusks	1
1866	Baird	Middle Province	Birds	1
1866	Grisebach	Prairie Region	Plants	1
1873	Cope	Central Region	Repts. and batrs.	2
1876	Wallace	Rocky Mountain Subregion.	Animals	2
1878	Allen	Middle Province	Animals	2
1881	Gray	Central Province	Plants	1
1883	Packard	Central Province	Animals	2
1883	Jordan	Central Region	Mollusks	3
1884	Drude	Montana District	Plants	2
1886	Hartlaub	Rocky Mountain Region	Birds	2
1887	Heilprin	Rocky Mountain Subregion.	Animals	2
1887	Brendel	Prairie Flora	Plants	1
1889	Ridgway	Rocky Mountain or Middle District.	Birds	2

Pacific or California Division.—This name has been very generally applied to the Pacific coast region of the United States. It was first recognized by the botanist De Candolle in 1820. Pickering, in 1830, named it the *Californian Flora*, but, knowing little or nothing of the Sierra Nevada and believing the Rocky Mountains to be the only mountain system of importance in North America, extended its eastern boundary to that range. In this he was followed by the botanist Hinds, in 1843; by the conchologists, Amos Binney, in 1851, and Woodward, in 1856. Agassiz, in 1854, was first to fix its eastern limit at the Sierra Nevada and Cascade mountains, where it has been permitted to rest. Its north and south boundaries have undergone considerable fluctuations.

The extent to which the Pacific or Californian region has been recognized will appear from the following table : *

Date	Author	Name given to region	Based on	Rank
1820	De Candolle	West Coast of Temperate North America.	Plants	1
1830	Pickering	Californian Flora	Plants	2
1843	Hinds	Californian Region	Plants	1
1848	Frankenheim	California	Plants	2
1851	Binney (A.)	Pacific Region	Mollusks	1
1854	Agassiz	Californian Fauna	Animals	3
1856	Woodward	Californian Province	Mollusks	1
1859	Le Conte	Western District	Insects	1
1859	Cooper	Nevadian Province†	Forests	1
1863	Binney (W. G.)	Pacific Province	Mollusks	1
1866	Baird	Western Province	Birds	1
1866	Grisebach	Californian Region	Plants	1
1873	Cope	Pacific Region	Repts. and batrchs.	2
1874	Porter	Pacific Region	Plants	1
1876	Wallace	Californian Subregion	Animals	2
1878	Allen	Western Province	Animals	2
1883	Packard	Western Province	Animals	1
1883	Jordan	Pacific Region	Mollusks	3
1884	Drude	Californian District	Plants	2
1886	Hartlaub	Californian Region	Birds	2
1887	Heilprin	Californian Subregion	Animals	2
1887	Brendel	Californian Flora	Plants	1
1889	Ridgway	Pacific District	Birds	2

* Engler's 'California Coast Province' is not included in this table, because it consists only of the narrow strip of land between the Coast Range and the Pacific.

† Named from the Sierra Nevada—not the State of Nevada.

Austroriparian or Louisianian Division.

(South Atlantic and Gulf States.)

Latreille, as early as 1817, called attention to the difference in the insect fauna of Carolina and Georgia from that of Pennsylvania and New York, and in his division of the earth into circumpolar zones ran the boundary line between these faunas at latitude 36°. The difference in the flora of the South Atlantic and Gulf States from that of the Northern States was recognized by the Danish botanist Schouw as early as 1822 in the ' *Realm of Magnolias, or Pursh's Realm,*' which he then proposed for the region between the parallels of 30° and 36° north latitude. Thirty-four years later (in 1856) the northern boundary of the same area was run by America's greatest botanist, Dr. Asa Gray, along the parallel of 36° 30', only half a degree from Schouw's line. The first zoologist to recognize this region was the elder Binney, who died in 1847. His posthumous work on *Terrestrial Air-Breathing Mollusks*, published in 1851, describes it under the name ' *Tertiary Region of the Atlantic Coast and the Gulf of Mexico.*' The elder Agassiz recognized it in 1854 as one of his seven primary regions, naming it the *Louisianian Fauna.* Later writers, except Cope, have considered it a subdivision of the Eastern Forest region. Cope restored it to primary rank in 1873 and named it the *Austroriparian Region.*

The extent to which this region has been recognized will appear from the following table:

Date	Author	Name given to region	Based on	Rank
1817	Latreille	Supertropical Climate...	Insects	1
1822	Schouw	Realm of Magnolias...	Plants	1
1836	Meyen	Subtropical Zone	Plants	1
1837	Martius	Mississippi-Floridian Realm.	Plants	1
1838	Berghaus	Realm of Magnolias....	Plants	1
1851	Binney (A.)	Tertiary Region of Atlantic and Gulf coasts.	Mollusks	2
1853	Schmarda	Middle American Realm.	Animals	1
1854	Agassiz	Louisianian Fauna	Animals	3
1856	Gray	Southern States	Plants	1
1859	Le Conte	Southern Province	Insects	2
1859	Cooper	Carolinian and Mississippian.	Forests	2
1863	Binney (W.G.)	Southern Region	Mollusks	2
1866	Baird	Southern Subdivision...	Birds	2
1866	Verrill	Louisianian Fauna	Birds	2
1871	Allen	Louisianian Fauna	Birds	3

Date	Author	Name given to region	Based on	Rank
1873	Cope	Austroriparian Region..	Repts. and batrchs.	2
1874	Porter	Southern District	Plants	2
1883	Jordan	Southern District	Mollusks	4
1884	Sargent	Coast Pine Region	Forests	2
1890	Merriam	Austroriparian Region..	Animals and plants.	2

Sonoran Division.

The term '*Sonoran Region*' has been applied by Cope and others to an important life area which enters the southwestern part of the United States from the table-land of Mexico. It was first recognized by a botanist, Richard Brinsley Hinds, R. N., surgeon to H. M. S. *Sulphur*, who published a description of it in 1843 under the name '*The Chihuahua Region.*' He defined it as extending south to the tropic, west to the Gulf of California and the Colorado River, north to the prairie region of the United States, and separated on the east from the Gulf of Mexico by a northward extension of the Central American region along the lowlands bordering the coast. Professor Baird (in 1866) stated that along the valleys of the Rio Grande and Gila the fauna of the Central Province "is greatly mixed up with the peculiar fauna of northern Mexico, which, as far as its summer birds indicate, is almost entitled to be considered as a fourth main province."

The extent to which this region has been recognized will appear from the following table:

Date	Author	Name given to region	Based on	Rank
1843	Hinds	Chihuahuan	Plants	1
1859	Le Conte	Southwestern and South-southwestern Provinces.	Insects	2
1859	Cooper	Arizonian Region	Forests	2
1861	Cooper	Arizonian and Chihuahuan Regions.	Forests	2
1866	Baird	[No name given]	Birds	2
1870	Brown	New Mexican Region	Forests	2
1873	Cope	Sonoran	Repts. and batrchs..	2
1874	Porter	Cactus Region	Plants	1
1878	Dyer	Mexico-Californian Flora	Plants	2
1882	Engler	Aztec Province	Plants	3
1884	Sargent	Mexican Forest Region	Forests	1
1884	Drude	North Mexico and Texas District.	Plants	2
1887	Heilprin	Sonoran Transition Region.	Animals	(?)
1890	Merriam	Sonoran Province	Animals and plants.	1

Peninsula of Lower California.

That the fauna and flora of the peninsula of Lower California, or any part of it, differs radically from that of the state of California immediately on the north was pointed out almost simultaneously by Baird and Le Conte in 1859. Baird stated that the fauna of its southern extremity, as determined by collections of its mammals, birds, and reptiles, "is almost identical with that of the Gila River, and to a certain extent with that of the Rio Grande," but differs wholly from that of Upper California. In accordance with these facts he afterward (in 1866) made Lower California a subdivision of the Central Province. Later in the same year (1859) Le Conte stated that a few species of insects from Cape St. Lucas, "though all new, indicate a greater resemblance to the fauna of the Lower Colorado than to that of maritime California; this province may therefore be found eventually to belong to the interior district."

Cooper (in 1861) proposed the name *Uchitan* for the Forest Flora of Lower California, and regarded it as a subdivision of his Nevadian (= Californian) Province. Grisebach also, in mapping the plant regions of the world in 1866, included the peninsula in his Californian Region, but afterward (in 1872) transferred it to the interior or prairie region.

Cope, in 1873, raised Lower California to primary rank, basing his action on a study of its reptiles and batrachians. Wallace, in 1876, placed it in the Central Province without subdivision. Packard, in 1883, followed Baird and Grisebach in regarding the southern part of the peninsula as a subdivision of the Central Province, while the northern part was assigned to the Pacific Province. Drude, in 1884, divided it transversely in two nearly equal plant areas, placing the northern half in his ' *North Mexico and Texas District,*' and the southern half in his tropical ' *Mexican District.*' Hartlaub and Newton, in 1886, placed the entire peninsula in their *Mexican Region*, and Heilprin, in 1887, in his *Sonoran Transition Region*.

The way in which Lower California has been regarded by different writers is shown in the following table: *

---

* NOTE.—In the few cases in which the peninsula has been divided, the assignment here given relates to the southern extremity.

Date	Author	How regarded	Study based on	Rank
1837	Martius	As part of his Mexican Extra-tropical Realm.	Plants	0
1838	Berghaus...	As part of his Mexican Realm ('Jacquin's Realm ').	Plants	0
1843	Hinds......	As part of his Californian Region.	Plants	0
1845	Berghaus...	As part of his Tropical Province.	Mammals	0
1854	Agassiz.....	As part of his Californian Fauna.	Animals	0
1856	Woodward .	As part of his Californian Province.	Mollusks	0
1859	Baird......	As a subdivision of his Middle Province.	Birds	2
1859	Le Conte...	As part of his Central District..	Insects	0
1861	Cooper.....	As a subdivision of his Nevadian [= Californian] Province.	Forests	2
1866	Grisebach..	As part of his Californian Region.	Plants	0
1870	Brown.....	As part of his Colorado Desert District.	Forests	0
1872	Grisebach..	As part of his Prairie Region...	Plants	0
1873	Cope.......	As an independent region......	Reptiles and batrachians.	2
1876	Wallace....	As part of his Californian Sub-region.	Animals	0
1882	Engler.....	As part of his Aztec Province..	Plants	0
1883	Packard....	As part of his Central Province.	Animals	0
1884	Drude......	As part of his Mexican District.	Plants	0
1886	Hartlaub...	As part of his Mexican Region.	Birds	0
1887	Heilprin....	As part of his Sonoran Transition Region.	Animals	0
1890	Merriam ...	As a division of his Sonoran Province.	Animals and plants.	2

Southern Florida.

The large number of tropical forms of life inhabiting southern Florida early led to its separation from the rest of the Atlantic region by writers on the distribution of animals and plants. Lesson (in 1831) placed it along with Mexico in his South Temperate Zone. Hinds (in 1843), recognizing its Antillean affinities, placed the southern extremity of the peninsula (south of latitude 27°) in his *West India Region.*

The extent to which southern Florida has been recognized as faunally and florally distinct from the rest of the United States is shown in the following table:

Date	Author	Name given to region	Based on	Rank
1831	Lesson	[Florida division of South Temperate Zone.]	Birds.......	0
1843	Hinds........	[Florida division of West India Region.]	Plants......	0
1851	Binney (A.) ..	Peninsula of Florida.........	Mollusks ...	2
1858	Cooper	Floridian Region..........,....	Forests	2
1859	Le Conte.....	Subtropical Province........	Insects	2
1866	Baird	[Florida division of Atlantic Region.]	Birds.......	3
1866	Verrill	[Florida division of West Indian Region.]	Birds.......	0
1870	Brown	Florida Subregion	Forests	2
1871	Allen	Floridian Fauna	Birds.......	3
1873	Cope.........	Floridian District	Reptiles and batrachians.	3
1874	Porter........	Florida Region	Plants......	1
1883	Packard......	[Florida division of Antillean Region.]	Animals....	0
1883	Jordan	[Florida division of Neotropical Province.]	Mollusks ...	0
1884	Sargent.......	Semi-tropical forest of Florida.	Forests	2
1887	Drude........	[Florida division of Antillean Region.]	Plants......	0
1887	Reichenow ...	[Florida division of South American Region.]	Birds.......	0
1887	Brendel	South Florida [Antillean] ...	Plants......	1
1888	Schwarz......	[Florida division of Antillean Region.]	Insects	0
1890	Merriam	[Florida division of Antillean Subregion.]	Animals and plants.	3

Antillean Division.

The fauna and flora of the West Indies have been variously interpreted by different writers, some placing the region in South America, others in Mexico, and others still raising it to independent rank.

In 1822 Schouw, in mapping the plant areas of the world, placed it in his '*Jacquin's Realm or Realm of Cactuses and Peppers,*' Subsequently, however (in 1833), he gave it independent primary rank, naming it '*Swartz's Realm.*' Martius, in 1837, was first to bestow the name '*Antillean Realm*' upon this region, which he regarded as a division of primary rank, comprising the West Indies and adjacent coasts of South and Central America. The same arrangement was retained in his lectures on Floral Realms in 1865.

The way in which the West Indies have been regarded by different writers is shown in the following table:

Date	Author	How regarded	Based on	Rank
1820	De Candolle	As an independent region	Plants	1
1822	Schouw	As part of his Realm of Cactuses and Peppers [Mexican].	Plants	0
1830	Pickering	As part of his American Intertropical Region.	Plants	0
1831	Lesson	As part of his Equatorial Zone.	Birds	0
1833	Schouw	As an independent realm (Swartz's Realm).	Plants	1
1835	De Candolle	As an independent region	Plants	1
1837	Martius	As an independent realm (Antillean Realm).	Plants	1
1838	Berghaus	As an independent realm (Swartz's Realm).	Plants	1
1841	Pompper	As part of his North Warm Zone.	Animals	0
1843	Hinds	As an independent realm (West India Region).	Plants	1
1845	Berghaus	As part of his Tropical Province.	Mammals	0
1846	Wagner	As part of his Tropical American Province.	Mammals	0
1854	Agassiz	As a subdivision of his Central American Region.	Animals	3
1856	Woodward	As an independent province (Antillean Province).	Mollusks	1
1858	Sclater	As part of his Neotropical Region.	Birds	0
1866	Baird	As a primary region (West Indian Region).	Birds	1
1866	Grisebach	As a primary region (West Indian Region).	Plants	1
1868	Huxley	As part of his Austro-Columbian Region.	Animals	0
1870	Brown	As an independent province (Antillean Province).	Forests	1
1875	Sclater	As an independent subregion (Antillean Subregion).	Birds	2
1876	Wallace	As an independent subregion (Antillean Subregion).	Animals	2
1882	Engler	As an independent province	Plants	3
1883	Packard	As an independent region (Antillean Region).	Animals	1
1883	Jordan	As part of his Neotropical Province.	Mollusks	0
1884	Drude	As an independent region (Antillean District).	Plants	2

Date	Author	How regarded	Based on	Rank
1886	Hartlaub	As an independent region (Antillean Region).	Birds.......	2
1887	Heilprin ... '.	As a subdivision of his Neo-tropical Region.	Animals....	2
1887	Reichenow ...	As part of his South American Region.	Birds.......	0
1890	Merriam	As a division of his Tropical Province.	Animals and plants.	2

Northwest Coast Division.

In 1843 Hinds, in mapping the plant regions of the world, proposed a ' *Northwest American Region* ' for the area west of the Rocky Mountains, north of the Columbia River, and south of latitude 68° north. Agassiz, in his paper on the Zoological regions of the earth (1854), gave the name ' *Northwest Coast Fauna* ' to essentially the same area (shown on his map as extending along the Pacific from northern California to the base of the Unalaskan peninsula).

In 1859 Le Conte, who based his studies on Coleoptera, spoke of this region as the ' *Hyperborean Province* ' of the Pacific district; and the same year Cooper, writing of forest regions, described it as the ' *Caurine Province.* ' W. G. Binney, in 1873, mentioned it as the ' *Oregonian Division* ' of the Pacific Province; Engler, in 1882, as the ' *Kaloschen Zone* '; Drude, in 1884, as the ' *Columbian District* '; Nelson, in 1887, as the ' *Sitkan District* '; Brendel, in 1887, as the ' *North Pacific Province.* '

Prairie Division.

A few botanists, influenced by the widely different aspects of nature resulting from the presence or absence of forests, have recognized a ' Prairie Region ' as one of the great floral divisions of North America. It was first proposed by Pickering, in 1830. Pickering named it the ' *Louisianian Flora,* ' and gave its boundaries as the Mississippi on the east and the Rocky Mountains on the west. Hinds described it, in 1843, as "a peculiar tract enclosed by the vast forests of North America." He named it the ' Prairie Region,' and said it extended "from within a hundred miles of the west bank of the Mississippi to the Rocky Mountains, stretching north to 54° north latitude, and again only bounded on the south by the wooded country of the Texas and the Mexican Sea."

Cooper, in his paper on the distribution of forests (in 1859), named it the *Campestrian Province.* It was recognized by Brown in 1870, by Porter in 1874, and by Engler in 1882.

RECAPITULATION.

It is seen that a number of zoologists and botanists, basing their studies on widely different groups, and as a rule ignorant of the writings of their predecessors, have agreed in the main in the recognition of at least seven (7) life areas in extratropical North America, namely: (1) an *Arctic area* north of the limit of tree growth; (2) a *Boreal transcontinental coniferous forest region;* (3) an *Atlantic or Eastern wooded region* stretching westward from the Atlantic to the Great Plains; (4) a *Central or Middle region,* reaching from the Plains to the Sierra Nevada and Cascade Mountains; (5) a *Pacific or Californian division,* covering the area between the east base of the Sierra and the Pacific ocean; (6) a Louisianian or *Austroriparian division,* comprising the South Atlantic and Gulf States south of latitude 36°; (7) a *Sonoran division,* occupying the high table-land of Mexico and stretching northward over the dry interior far enough to include the southern parts of California, Nevada, Arizona, New Mexico, and Texas.

With or without reference to the above principal divisions, it has been recently the custom of zoologists, particularly ornithologists, to subdivide the eastern United States and Canada into several minor areas or 'faunas,' as follows: (*a*) Floridian; (*b*) Louisianian; (*c*) Carolinian; (*d*) Alleghanian; (*e*) Canadian; (*f*) Hudsonian; and (*g*) Arctic. Of these the Canadian and Hudsonian form a part of the '*Boreal*' region above mentioned, and the Floridian and Louisianian together make up the '*Austroriparian*' division, leaving only the Carolinian and Alleghanian for the so-called 'Eastern Province' to rest on. The true relations of these zones will be explained later.

LIFE REGIONS AND ZONES OF NORTH AMERICA.

In a communication I had the honor to lay before this Society two years ago (December 4, 1889) * I stated that the Hudsonian

---

* Since published in my report on the "*Results of a Biological Survey of the San Francisco Mountain Region in Arizona,*" N. Am. Fauna, No. 3, September 11, 1890.

and Canadian zones of the East belong to the *Boreal* region and extend completely across the continent, and that the desert areas of the West belong to the Southern or *Sonoran* region. The pine plateau (*Pinus ponderosa*) of Arizona and other parts of the West was "shown to consist of a mixture of Boreal and Sonoran types. * . * * In other words, it is *neutral* territory" (North American Fauna, No. 3, September, 1890, p. 20). I remarked further that the Carolinian fauna "is suffused with southern forms, and the Alleghanian seems to be *neutral* ground" (Ibid. p. 18), thus implying that the 'neutral' or pine-plateau zone of Arizona is the western equivalent of the 'Alleghanian Fauna' of the East.

In a subsequent publication (North American Fauna, No. 5, August, 1891) I went a step further, defining the treeless parts of the 'Neutral or Transition Zone,' and characterizing an 'Upper Sonoran Zone' as distinguished from the Lower or True Sonoran; but nothing was said as to the relations of these zones with those long recognized in the East.

The time has now arrived, however, when it is possible to correlate the Sonoran Zones of the West with corresponding zones in the East, as was done two years ago in the case of the Boreal Zones, and as was intimated in the case of the Neutral or Transition Zone. It can now be asserted with some confidence not only that the Transition Zone of the West is the equivalent of the Alleghanian of the East, but also that the Upper Sonoran is the equivalent of the Carolinian, and the Lower Sonoran of the Austroriparian, and that each can be traced completely across the continent. Thus, all the major and minor zones that have been established in the East are found to be uninterruptedly continuous with corresponding zones in the West, though their courses are often tortuous, following the lines of equal temperature during the season of reproduction, which lines conform in a general way to the contours of altitude, rising with increased base-level and falling with increased latitude.

The BOREAL REGION extends obliquely across the entire continent from New England and Newfoundland to Alaska and British Columbia, and from about latitude 45° north to the Polar Sea, conforming in general direction to the trend of the northern shores of the continent. It recedes to about latitude 54° on the plains of the Saskatchewan, and gives off three long arms or chains of islands, which reach far south along the three great mountain systems of the United States—an eastern arm in the

Alleghanies, a central arm in the Rocky Mountains, and a western arm in the Cascades and Sierra Nevada. The latter at its northern base occupies the entire breadth of the Pacific Coast region from the eastern slope of the mountains to the sea, but in passing southward bifurcates, the main fork following the lofty Cascade and Sierra ranges to about latitude 36°; the other following the coast, gradually losing its distinctive characters and becoming invaded with Sonoran forms until it disappears a little north of San Francisco.

The following genera of mammals belong exclusively to the Boreal Region, none of them ranging south beyond the Transition Zone:

Cervus	Cuniculus
Rangifer	Zapus
Alce	Erethizon
Mazama	Lagomys
Ovibos	Thalarctos
Arctomys	Latax
Aplodontia	Gulo
Evotomys	Mustela
Phenacomys	Neurotrichus (?)
Myodes	Condylura

In addition to the above, the following genera are clearly of Boreal origin, although reaching and in some cases penetrating parts of the Sonoran Region:

Ovis	Vulpes
Bison *	Ursus
Tamias	Lutreola
Castor	Putorius
Arvicola	Sorex
Fiber	

Besides the genera here enumerated, the following subgenera belong to the Boreal Region: *Tamiasciurus* (containing the red or spruce squirrels), *Mynomes* and *Chilotus* (field-mice or voles, of which *Mynomes* reaches south a little beyond the Transition Zone), *Teonoma* (the bushy-tailed wood-rats), and *Neosorex* and *Atophyrax* (subgenera of shrews).

---

* The faunal position of the genus *Bison* is not so certain as in the case of the other genera here mentioned, though both the American and the European species seem to be of Boreal origin.

The Boreal Region is made up of two principal divisions, both circumpolar: (1) An *Arctic division*, above the limit of tree growth; and (2) A *Boreal Coniferous Forest division*.

Arctic Mammals.

(Found above the limit of trees and all circumpolar.)

A. *Exclusively Arctic.*

Eskimo	*Homo*
Polar bear	*Thalarctos maritimus*
Barren ground bear	*Ursus richardsoni*
Musk ox	*Ovibos moschatus*
Barren ground caribou	*Rangifer grœnlandicus*
Arctic fox	*Vulpes lagopus*
Arctic hare	*Lepus glacialis*
Lemming	*Myodes obensis*
Lemming	*Cuniculus torquatus*
Arctic red-backed mouse	*Evotomys rutilus*
Parry's spermophile	*Spermophilus empetra*

B. *Common to Arctic and Hudsonian.*

Wolverine	*Gulo luscus*
Gray wolf	*Canis griseus*
Ermine	*Putorius erminea*

The *Boreal Coniferous Forest division* may be subdivided into at least two transcontinental zones: (*a*) Hudsonian, and (*b*) Canadian; and a third or 'Timberline Zone' may be differentiated from the Hudsonian proper. In speaking of the divisions of the Boreal Region on high mountains it is customary to add the word *alpine* to the name of the division; thus, *Arctic-alpine, Hudsonian-alpine,* and so on.

Mammals of the Boreal Zone.

(The letter *a* indicates that the species is known only from mountains, or is an alpine form.)

Cervus canadensis	Sciurus fremonti
Rangifer caribou	mogollonensis (*a*)
Alce americanus	hudsonicus
Mazama montana	californicus (*a*)
Ovis canadensis	vancouverensis
dalli	richardsoni
Sciuropterus volans sabrinus	douglassi

Tamias cinereicollis (*a*)
   obscurus (*a*)
   senex (*a*)
   speciosus (*a*)
   townsendi
   umbrinus (*a*)
   quadrivittatus (*a*)
      amœnus (*a*)
      luteiventris (*a*)
      borealis
      neglectus
Spermophilus lateralis
   castanurus (*a*)
   chrysodeirus (*a*)
   cinerascens
   armatus (*a*)
   beldingi (*a*)
   empetra
      kodiacensis
   columbianus
Arctomys caligatus (*a*)
   dacota (*a*)
   flaviventer (*a*)
Aplodontia major (*a*)
   rufa
Sitomys americanus arcticus
   austerus
Neotoma cinerea drummondi
Phenacomys borealis
   celatus
   intermedius
   latimanus
   longicaudus·
   orophilus (*a*)
   . ungava
Evotomys californicus
   occidentalis
   idahoensis
   carolinensis (*a*)
   dawsoni
   galei (*a*)
   gapperi
      brevicaudus
Arvicola alticolus (*a*)

Arvicola drummondi
   nanus (*a*)
   oregonus
   mordax
   longicaudus
   townsendi
   macropus
   xanthognathus
Myodes obensis
Cuniculus torquatus
Zapus hudsonius
Erethizon dorsatus
   epixanthus
Lagomys princeps (*a*)
   schisticeps (*a*)
Lepus americanus
   bairdii (*a*)
   washingtoni
Lynx canadensis
Ursus americanus
   horribilis
Putorius culbertsoni
   longicauda
Mustela americana
   caurina
   pennanti
Sorex belli
   dobsoni (*a*)
   forsteri
   idahoensis
   monticolus (*a*)
   pacificus
   richardsoni
   sphagnicolus
   suckleyi
   trowbridgei
   vagrans
      similis (*a*)
   albibarbis
   palustris
   hydrodromus
Condylura cristata
Vesperugo noctivagans
Atalapha cinerea

The SONORAN REGION as a whole stretches across the continent from Atlantic to Pacific, covering nearly the whole country south of latitude 43° and reaching northward on the Great Plains and Great Basin to about latitude 48°. It is invaded from the north by three principal intrusions of Boreal forms along the three great mountain systems already mentioned; while to the southward it occupies the great interior basin of Mexico and extends into the tropics along the highlands of the interior. It covers also the peninsula of Lower California, the southern part of which seems entitled to rank as an independent subdivision.

The following genera belong exclusively to the Sonoran Region (as distinguished from the Boreal), none of them ranging north beyond the Transition Zone. Those preceded by the letter *T* are intrusions from the Tropical Region.

T Didelphis	Bassariscus
T Tatusia	*T* Nasua
T Dicotyles	Conepatus
Reithrodontomys *	Spilogale
Onychomys	Notiosorex
Oryzomys	Scalops
Sigmodon	Corynorhinus
Geomys	Euderma
Dipodomys	Antrozous
Perodipus †	Nycticejus
Microdipodops	*T* Molossus
Perognathus	*T* Nyctinomus
Heteromys	*T* Otopterus
Urocyon	

In addition to the above, the following genera seem to be of Sonoran or austral origin, although reaching and in some cases penetrating a considerable distance into the Boreal region:

*The generic name *Reithrodontomys* was proposed by Giglioli in 1873 (Richerche intorno alla Distribuzione Geografica Generale, Roma, 1873, p. 160), and antedates *Ochetodon* of Coues.

† The generic name *Perodipus* was proposed in 1867 by Fitzinger for the five-toed kangaroo rats (Sitzungsber. math. nat. Classe, K. Akad. Wiss. Wien, LVI, 1867, p. 126), thus antedating by twenty-three years the name *Dipodops* proposed by the writer for the same type in 1890 (North Am. Fauna, No. 3, September, 1890, p. 72). Both generic names were based on *Dipodomys agilis* of Gambel, from Los Angeles, California.

Cariacus	Mephitis
Antilocapra	T Felis
Cynomys	Lynx
Sitomys *	Scapanus
Neotoma	Blarina
Thomomys	Atalapha
T Procyon	Vesperugo
Taxidea	Vespertilio

The genera *Sitomys*, *Mephitis*, *Lynx*, *Atalapha*, *Vesperugo*, and *Vespertilio* range well north in the Boreal Zone, where each is represented by a single species. In the Sonoran Zone, on the other hand, these same genera reach their maximum development and are represented by numerous species.

Besides the genera above enumerated, a number of subgenera belong to the Sonoran Region. Among these are *Neosciurus* and *Parasciurus* (subgenera of *Sciurus*), *Xerospermophilus*,† *Ammospermophilus*‡ and *Ictidomys* (subgenera of *Spermophilus*), *Pitymys*, *Pedomys* and *Neofiber* (subgenera of *Arvicola*), and *Chætodipus* (a subgenus of *Perognathus*, which is almost entitled to rank as a full genus).

The Sonoran Region may be divided by temperature into two principal transcontinental zones, (*a*) *Upper Sonoran*, and (*b*) *Lower Sonoran;* § and each of these in turn may be subdivided into *arid* and *humid* divisions.

The gray fox, *Urocyon*, ranges over both Upper and Lower Sonoran from Atlantic to Pacific; and pocket gophers of the

---

* The generic name *Hesperomys* being untenable, Allen has recently substituted for it the name *Vesperimus*, proposed by Coues as a subgenus in 1874 (Bull. Am. Mus. Nat. Hist., III, No. 2, June, 1891, pp. 291-297). *Vesperimus* is antedated by *Sitomys* of Fitzinger, proposed in 1867, and based on Gapper's *Cricetus myoides* from Lake Simcoe, Ontario, Canada (Sitzungsber. math. nat. Classe, K. Akad. Wiss. Wien, LVI, 1867, p. 97). Gapper's *Cricetus myoides* is the common white-footed mouse of southern Ontario and northern New York, which therefore becomes the type of the genus.

† *Xerospermophilus*, subgen. nov., proposed for *Spermophilus mohavensis* (type) and the allied species of the *S. spilosoma* group.

‡ *Ammospermophilus*, subgen. nov., proposed for *Spermophilus leucurus* (type) and allied species.

§ The great Lower Sonoran Zone may be split lengthwise (in an east and west direction) into two belts which have not yet been thoroughly differentiated.

genus *Geomys* inhabit both these divisions on the Great Plains and in the Mississippi Valley, and range east to the Atlantic in the Austroriparian Zone.

Both divisions of the Lower Sonoran are inhabited by the transcontinental genera *Reithrodontomys*, *Sigmodon*, *Corynorhinus*, *Nyctinomus*, *Otopterus*, *Neotoma*, and *Spilogale*, though in the west the two last mentioned range through the Upper Sonoran also.

The humid Lower Sonoran or *Austroriparian* is a division of much importance. It begins on the Atlantic seaboard at the mouth of Chesapeake Bay and stretches thence southwesterly, embracing the alluvial lands of the South Atlantic and Gulf States below what geologists know as the ' fall line,' rising in the Mississippi bottom as far as the junction of the Ohio with the Mississippi, and following the former in a narrow strip to the point where it receives the Wabash. On the west side of the Mississippi it crosses Arkansas, reaches southern Missouri and southeastern Kansas, and spreads out over Indian and Oklohoma Territories and Texas, where it loses its moisture and merges insensibly into the arid Sonoran. *Oryzomys* and *Nycticejus* are distinctive Austroriparian genera. Six other genera (*Neotoma*, *Reithrodontomys*, *Geomys*, *Spilogale*, *Nyctinomus*, and *Corynorhinus*), which in the region east of the Mississippi seem to be restricted to this division, have a more extended range in the west. The cotton rat (*Sigmodon*), another characteristic Austroriparian genus. has a very limited range in the arid Sonoran.

The arid Lower Sonoran extends westerly from the humid Sonoran to the Pacific, covering southern New Mexico and Arizona south of the plateau rim (sending a tongue up the Rio Grande to a point above Albuquerque), the west side of which it follows northerly to the extreme northwestern corner of Arizona and the southwestern corner of Utah (where it is restricted to the valley of the lower Santa Clara, or St. George Valley), and thence westerly across Nevada, reaching northerly to Pahranagat, Oasis, and Owens Valleys, and thence curving southwesterly, following the eastern base of the Sierra Nevada, Tehachapi, and Tejon Mountains. and covers the whole of the Mohave and Colorado Deserts and all the rest of southern California except the mountains. It sends an arm southward over most of the peninsula of Lower California, and another northward covering the San Joaquin and Sacramento Valleys. The distinctive mammals of the arid Lower Sonoran are kangaroo rats of the genus *Dipodomys*, pocket mice of the subgenus *Chætodipus*, and spermophiles of the subgenera *Xerospermophilus* and *Ammospermophilus*.

The peninsula of Lower California is a subdivision of the arid Lower Sonoran Zone. Not a single genus of land mammal or bird is restricted to it and but two peculiar species of mammals have been described. The peculiar birds are more numerous, but with few exceptions are only subspecifically separable from those of neighboring parts of the United States and Mexico. They may be classed in two categories: (1) Mountain forms derived from the North (of Boreal or Transition origin); and (2) lowland forms derived from the contiguous plains (of Sonoran, or in one instance subtropical, origin). As would be expected from the character of the country, the great majority are subspecies of well-known Sonoran forms, with the addition of a small number of peculiar species belonging to Sonoran genera. But a single subtropical bird is known, namely, *Dendroica bryanti castaneiceps*, and it is restricted to the mangrove lagoons.

The presence of this subtropical bird in the narrow coast lagoons is in complete accord with the vegetation of the coast strip, which, as Mr. T. S. Brandegee tells us, is subtropical.[*] This indicates the presence of a narrow coast belt similar to that of southern Florida, but of less extent. It is possible that *Basilinna xantusi* is subtropical rather than Sonoran, but the details of distribution of the genus are not well known.

Among reptiles, about 25 peculiar species of snakes and lizards are believed to be restricted to the peninsula, but no peculiar genus is known. Three of the genera are tropical, and nine are arid Lower Sonoran.

In addition to the peculiar species and subspecies of the peninsula, many characteristic arid Lower Sonoran forms of mammals, birds, reptiles, insects, and plants abound. Among the latter may be mentioned the highly distinctive Sonoran desert brush, *Larrea mexicana* and *Krameria parvifolia*.

Cope includes the whole peninsula in his *Lower Californian Region*, but other writers restrict the peculiar fauna and flora to the end of the peninsula south of the north foot of the mountains between La Paz and Todos Santos. Bryant states: "There is no more sharply defined faunal and floral area, that occurs to

---

[*] Brandegee, Proc. Calif. Acad. Sci., 2d ser., III, 1891, 110.

me now, excepting that of islands, than is embraced in the region above defined,"* but he omits to name the forms by which it is characterized. It is evident, however, that the peculiar fauna of the peninsula of Lower California entitles it to rank as a minor subdivision of the Lower Sonoran Zone. It is in effect an insular fauna of recent origin, bearing the same relation to that of the mainland as do several of the adjacent islands.

The humid division of the Upper Sonoran comprises the area in the eastern United States commonly known as the Carolinian Fauna. The opossum (*Didelphis*) here finds its northern limit, as do the so-called pine mouse (subgenus *Pitymys*) and the Georgian bat (*Vesperugo georgianus*). Before reaching the 100th meridian this area gradually loses its moisture and spreads out over the Great Plains as the arid or true Upper Sonoran, reaching an altitude of about 4,000 feet along the east foot of the Rocky Mountains in the latitude of Colorado, and sending a tongue northward along the Missouri obliquely through North Dakota and into eastern Montana. Another subdivision of the arid Upper Sonoran occupies the greater part of the Great Basin between the Rocky Mountains and the High Sierra, reaching northerly from the upper border of the Lower Sonoran to and including the plains of the Columbia and Snake Rivers. Another part of noteworthy extent is a narrow belt encircling the interior basin of California—the valley of the Sacramento and San Joaquin rivers—and a branch of the same along the coast between Monterey and the Santa Barbara plain. The following genera of mammals find their northern limit in the arid Upper Sonoran Zone: *Perodipus, Microdipodops, Perognathus, Onychomys, Spilogale, Urocyon, Bassariscus,* and *Antrozous.*

Interposed between the Boreal and Sonoran Regions throughout their numerous windings and interdigitations, is the Neutral or Transition Zone. The humid division of this zone, known as the Alleghanian Fauna,† covers the greater part of New

---

* Walter E. Bryant in Zoe, II, No. 3, Oct., 1891, 186. See also his important 'Catalogue of the Birds of Lower California,' Proc. Calif. Acad. Sci., 2d ser., II, 1889, 237–320.

† Prof. Louis Agassiz, in his highly important work on Lake Superior, clearly recognized the transition nature of this zone, for he says: "The State of Massachusetts, with its long arm stretched into the ocean eastward, or rather the region extending westward under the same parallel through the State of New York, forms a natural limit between the vegeta-

England (except Maine and the mountains of Vermont and New Hampshire) and extends westerly over the greater part of New York, southern Ontario, and Pennsylvania, and sends an arm south along the Alleghanies all the way across the Virginias, Carolinas, and eastern Tennessee, to northern Georgia and Alabama. In the Great Lake region this zone continues westerly across southern Michigan and Wisconsin, and then curves northward over the prairie region of Minnesota, covering the greater parts of North Dakota, Manitoba, and the plains of the Saskatchewan; thence bending abruptly south, it crosses eastern Montana and Wyoming, including parts of western South Dakota and Nebraska, and forms a belt along the eastern base of the Rocky Mountains in Colorado and northern New Mexico, here as elsewhere occupying the interval between the Upper Sonoran and Boreal Zones.

In Wyoming the Transition Zone passes broadly over the well-known low divide of the Rocky Mountains, which affords the route of the Union Pacific railway, and is directly continuous with the same zone in parts of Colorado, Utah, and Idaho, skirting the Boreal boundaries of the Great Basin all the way around the plains of the Columbia, sending an arm northward over the dry interior of British Columbia, descending along the eastern base of the Cascade Range and the High Sierra to the southern extremity of the latter, and occupying the summits of the Coast Ranges in California and of many of the desert ranges of the Great Basin.

The Transition Zone, as its name indicates, is a zone of overlapping of Boreal and Sonoran types. Many Boreal genera and species here reach the extreme southern limits of their distribution, and many Sonoran genera and species their northern limits. But a single mammalian genus (*Synaptomys*) is restricted to the Transition Zone, and future research may show it to inhabit the Boreal Region also.

---

tion of the warm temperate zone and that of the cold temperate zone. * * * Not only is this also the northern limit of the culture of fruit trees, but this zone is equally remarkable for the great variety of elegant shrubs which occur particularly on its northern borders, where we find so great a variety of species belonging to the genera, Celastrus, Cratægus, Ribes, Cornus, Hamamelis, Vaccinium, Kalmia, Rhodora, Azalea, Rhododendron, Andromeda, Clethra, Viburnum, Cephalanthus, Prinos, Dirca, Celtis, &c." (Lake Superior, 1850, 182-183.)

The following Boreal genera of mammals disappear in the Transition Zone·

Tamias *	Vulpes *
Fiber †	Cervus
Evotomys	Ovis *
Zapus	Ursus *
Erethizon	Neurotrichus
Arctomys	Condylura

The following Sonoran genera of mammals disappear in the Transition Zone:

Antilocapra	Perognathus
Cynomys	Bassariscus ‡
Spilogale ‡	Urocyon ‡
Geomys	Scalops
Thomomys ₰	

As already stated, the only mammalian genus apparently restricted to the Transition Zone is *Synaptomys*—a lemming mouse. A number of species, however, seem to be nearly or quite confined to this zone. Among these are the following:

Sciurus aberti	Spermophilus spilosoma pratensis
fossor ‖	grammurus
carolinensis leucotis	townsendi ‖
Tamias merriami	Cynomys leucurus
minimus	Sitomys nebrascensis
pictus	boylii
striatus	michiganensis
Spermophilus elegans	Arvicola mogollonensis
richardsoni	austerus minor
obsoletus	curtatus

---

* Except one species, which inhabits a limited part of the Sonoran Region.

† *Fiber* ranges south beyond the normal limit of the Transition Zone, but it does so along the banks of cool streams that give it a much lower temperature than that of the surrounding atmosphere. It is probable that both *Fiber* and *Castor* should be classed with aquatic species, the limits of their distribution depending on the temperature of the water. The same is true in a less degree of the paludal subgenera *Neosorex* and *Atophyrax* (of *Sorex*) and of the semi-amphibious members of the subgenus *Mynomes* (of *Arvicola*).

‡ These genera barely enter the Transition Zone at all except in a very small area in the far West.

₰ Except on high mountains in the Sonoran Region.

‖ Range down into Upper Sonoran also.

Arvicola pallidus
Synaptomys cooperi
Lepus americanus virginianus
    campestris
    idahoensis *
    sylvaticus nuttalli *

Perognathus fasciatus
    olivaceous
Putorius nigripes *
Vulpes velox
Scapanus americanus
Vespertilio melanorhinus

Local elevations of the land in the Sonoran Region are capped with isolated patches of Transition or Boreal species, according to the temperature to which their summits attain; and if the elevation is sufficient to secure a Boreal fauna and flora the latter is always separated from the Sonoran of the surrounding plane by a belt or girdle of Transition Zone forms.

The TROPICAL REGION reaches the United States at two remote points—Florida and Texas. In the former it exists as a narrow subtropical belt encircling the southern half of the Peninsula from Cape Malabar on the east to Tampa Bay on the west. In Texas it crosses the Lower Rio Grande from Mexico and extends north to the neighborhood of the Nueces River. In western Mexico the Tropical Region reaches Mazatlan.

Fourteen families of Tropical mammals inhabit North America north of Panama, namely:

Didelphidæ
Bradypodidæ
Myrmecophagidæ
Dasypodidæ
Dicotylidæ
Tapiridæ
Octodontidæ

Dasyproctidæ
Procyonidæ
Solenodontidæ
Emballonuridæ
Phyllostomatidæ
Hapalidæ
Cebidæ

Of the above fourteen families, six reach the United States, namely, *Didelphidæ, Dasypodidæ, Dicotylidæ, Procyonidæ, Emballonuridæ*, and *Phyllostomatidæ*, and two of the latter (*Didelphidæ* and *Procyonidæ*) penetrate the entire breadth of the Sonoran Region, the *Procyonidæ* even entering the lower edge of the Boreal. Descending from families to genera, it is found that no less than 62 tropical genera of non-pelagic mammals inhabit North America north of Panama, of which number 9 enter the United States from Mexico, namely, *Didelphis, Tatusia, Dicotyles, Nasua, Procyon, Felis, Molossus, Nyctinomus*, and *Otopterus*. Of these, *Didelphis, Felis*, and *Procyon* now reach considerably further north than the others, as just pointed out in speaking of the

---

* Range down into Upper Sonoran also.

families to which they respectively belong. In explanation of this extended range it is found that these genera inhabited North America in pre-glacial times and as a consequence have become acclimatized to a wider range of climatic conditions. The semi-Tropical belt of Florida is not known to possess any tropical mammals except bats and a large indigenous mouse (*Sitomys macropus*)*, but it has not been explored by experienced mammal collectors. Still, its recent origin and complete isolation from other tropical areas would indicate the absence of terrestrial species derived from the south. At the same time it is known to be rich in tropical plants, land shells, insects, and birds, as is shown in another part of the present paper (see pp. 51–53). It contains 9 genera of tropical birds, namely, *Zenaida, Geotrygon, Starnœnas, Rostrhamus, Polyborus, Crotophaga, Euetheia, Callichelidon,* and *Cœreba*.

The following 62 genera of mammals belong to the North American Tropical Region. The nine preceded by the letter *S* enter the southern United States, which they penetrate varying distances. *Nyctinomus* and *Otopterus* inhabit the Lower Sonoran Zone in common with the Tropical; *Didelphis* pushes completely through the humid division of the Sonoran Region; and *Felis* and *Procyon* enter the lower edge of the Boreal.

NORTH AMERICAN TROPICAL GENERA.

Chironectes	*S* Felis	Lonchorhina
S Didelphis	*S* Procyon	*S* Otopterus
Bradypus	Bassaricyon	Vampyrus
Cholœpus	*S* Nasua	Micronycteris
Myrmecophaga	Cercoleptes	Trachyops
Tamandua	Galictis	Phyllostoma
Cycloturas	Solenodon	Mimon
S Tatusia	Natalus	Hemiderma
S Dicotyles	Rhynchonycteris	Glossophaga
Elasmognathus	Saccopteryx	Phyllonycteris
Capromys	Diclidurus	Monophylla
Plagiodontia	Noctilio	Leptonycteris
Echinomys	*S* Molossus	Glossonycteris
Synetheres	*S* Nyctinomus	Chœronycteris
Dasyprocta	Chilonycteris	Artibeus
Cœlogenys	Mormops	Vampyrops

* Described by the writer as *Hesperomys macropus* in N. Am. Fauna, No. 4, Oct., 1890, p. 53.

Stenoderma	Centurio	Chrysothrix
Chiroderma	Desmodus	Nyctipithecus
Pygoderma	Diphylla	Ateles
Sturnira	Midas	Cebus
Brachyphylla	Mycetes	

Recapitulating, it is found that of the one hundred and thirty four genera of non-pelagic mammals inhabiting North America north of Panama, fifty-three are exclusively Tropical, twenty exclusively Sonoran, and twenty exclusively Boreal. In addition to these genera, which do not outstep the limits of the regions to which they severally belong, a number of others are clearly referable to the same regions, though ranging varying distances beyond their proper boundaries. Including these genera, the number belonging to each region is as follows: Tropical, sixty-two; Sonoran, thirty-four; Boreal, thirty-one—thus leaving but seven genera out of a total of one hundred and thirty-four that are not distinctly referable to one of the three regions. One of these (*Synaptomys*) is not known to occur outside the limits of the Transition Zone, leaving but six genera that have not been assigned. These genera are *Sciuropterus*, *Sciurus*, *Spermophilus*, *Lepus*, *Canis*, and *Lutra*, each of which ranges over large parts of both Boreal and Sonoran Regions. All except *Spermophilus* inhabit the Tropical Region also, and all are of great antiquity, as will be shown presently (p. 37). The genera *Spermophilus* and *Lepus* might be referred to the Sonoran Region because the great majority of their species are confined to it; and for the same reason *Sciurus* might be considered Tropical and Sonoran.

Omitting Mexico and Central America, and regarding the nine intrusive Tropical genera already mentioned as Sonoran (in contradistinction to Boreal), it is found that eighty-one genera of non-pelagic mammals inhabit the United States and Canada, of which forty-three may be looked upon as of Sonoran origin and thirty-one as of Boreal origin. The seven genera remaining are those mentioned in the last paragraph.

TABLE SHOWING THE GEOGRAPHIC DISTRIBUTION OF NORTH AMERICAN GENERA OF NON-PELAGIC MAMMALS OCCURRING NORTH OF MEXICO.

Boreal Genera.

Cervus	Arvicola *	Ursus *
Rangifer	Fiber *	Thalarctos
Alce	Evotomys	Latax
Ovis *	Phenacomys	Gulo
Mazama	Myodes	Mustela
Bison (?)	Cuniculus	Lutreola *
Ovibos	Zapus	Putorius *
Tamias *	Erethizon	Sorex*
Arctomys	Lagomys	Neurotrichus (?)
Aplodontia	Vulpes*	Condylura
Castor *		

Sonoran Genera.

Cariacus †	Perodipus	Notiosorex
Antilocapra	Microdipodops	Blarina†
Cynomys	Perognathus	Scapanus
Reithrodontomys	Heteromys	Scalops
Onychomys	Lynx †	Corynorhinus
Sitomys†	Urocyon	Euderma
Oryzomys	Bassariscus	Antrozous
Sigmodon	Taxidea	Nycticejus
Neotoma †	Conepatus	Vesperugo †
Geomys	Mephitis †	Atalapha †
Thomomys	Spilogale	Vespertilio †
Dipodomys		

Tropical Genera.

Didelphis	Felis †	Molossus
Tatusia	Procyon †	Nyctinomus
Dicotyles	Nasua	Otopterus

Transition Zone Genera.

Synaptomys

Genera Inhabiting both Boreal and Sonoran Zones.

Sciuropterus	Spermophilus	Lutra
Sciurus	Canis	Lepus

* Having one species in Sonoran Zone or reaching Sonoran.
† Having one species in Boreal Zone or reaching southern edge of Boreal.

DISTINCTNESS OF THE TROPICAL REGION FROM THE SONORAN.

It has been shown that the fauna and flora of Tropical America reach the United States, though in a somewhat dilute condition, along the lower Rio Grande in Texas, and in southern Florida, and that in the vast majority of cases their genera and species differ widely from those of other parts of America. Except for the presence, chiefly in the southern United States, of a comparatively few forms derived from the Tropical region, the fauna and flora of North America are as distinctive and independent of the existence of this area as if separated from it by the broad ocean. Among the eighty-one genera of non-pelagic *Mammalia* inhabiting North America north of Mexico the number of these intrusive genera is only nine,* as has been shown, and three of these are bats. . These genera are: *Didelphis, Tatusia, Dicotyles, Felis, Procyon, Nasua, Molossus, Nyctinomus,* and *Otopterus. Tatusia* and *Nasua* barely reach our southern boundary; *Dicotyles* extends only part way through Texas; *Molossus* a short distance into southern California; *Nyctinomus* and *Otopterus* do not pass beyond the Lower Sonoran Zone, and *Didelphis* is restricted to the humid division of the Sonoran. Out of the nine intrusive genera, therefore, but two (*Felis* and *Procyon*) reach the southern edge of the Boreal.

On the other hand, a few groups, such as the wolves, otters, squirrels, and rabbits (genera *Canis, Lutra, Sciurus, Sciuropterus, Spermophilus,* and *Lepus*) occur over large parts of both North and South America, presenting a seeming obstacle to the acceptance of the view that the faunas in question are so wholly dissimilar. But investigation shows that these animals are almost world-wide in distribution, implying great antiquity of origin, and remains of most of them have been found as low down at least as the Miocene strata in both America and Eurasia. Hence it is clear that these types became diffused over North and South America at a very distant period, and their peculiar habits of life, though wholly dissimilar, enabled them to survive the great mutations these land areas have undergone since Miocene times.

The paucity of species of tropical derivation in North America is the more remarkable in view of the absence of barriers of any kind, save climatic conditions alone, to impede the free in-

*Among birds the number of intrusive forms is greater, as would be expected from their superior powers of locomotion and dispersion.

gress of species from the south. No mountain range or arm of the sea or other tangible obstacle marks the northern boundary of the semi-tropical fauna of northeastern Mexico where it ends abruptly near the Nueces River in Texas, or the semi-tropical belt of Florida where it ends near Tampa Bay on the west and Cape Malabar on the east.

If the Tropical fauna and flora stopped at the narrow Isthmus of Panamá, or even in southern Nicaragua, where the last union of the North and South American continents probably took place, the case would be very different; but instead of doing this it pushes northward 1,500-2,000 miles and ends abruptly where the most painstaking search fails to reveal any barrier to further extension except an uncongenial decrease in temperature and humidity (see also remarks under change of climate following Pleistocene times p. 44.)

No more striking illustration could be desired of the potency of climate compared with the inefficiency of physical barriers than is presented by the almost total dissimilarity of the North American Tropical and Sonoran Regions, though in direct contact, contrasted with the great similarity of the Boreal Regions of North America and Eurasia—now separated by broad oceans, though formerly united, doubtless, in the region of Bering Sea. Of the thirty-one Boreal genera of North American mammals all but eight, or three-fourths, occur also in Eurasia, and but a single family is restricted to cold-temperate America. This family (the *Aplodontidæ*) is the sole representative of a group approaching extinction, and the accident of its survival (in a single genus and two closely related species) in a very limited area along our west coast can hardly be construed as of much faunal significance. Contrasted with this one family (which ought not to be counted) and eight genera of Boreal North American mammals not occurring in Eurasia, Tropical North America (Central America and part of Mexico, exclusive of the West Indies) has no less than eight families and fifty-three genera not belonging to the immediately adjoining Sonoran Region of the southern United States and the plateau of Mexico.

The Sonoran not a Transition Region.

Before leaving this part of the subject reference should be made to the view recently advanced by some naturalists, notably by

Angelo Heilprin, that the Sonoran Region is itself a 'Transition Region' between the Boreal and Tropical Faunas and Floras. The incorrectness of this hypothesis is easily demonstrated, for it rests upon the assumption that the Sonoran Region is a mixture of Boreal and Tropical forms. The contrary has just been shown to be the case, the hiatus between the Sonoran and Boreal on the one hand and the Sonoran and Tropical on the other being not only immense, but vastly greater than that between Boreal America and Eurasia.

DIFFERENTIATION OF LIFE FROM THE NORTH SOUTHWARD.

Animals and plants inhabiting the Arctic regions are usually specifically identical throughout Arctic America, Greenland, and the polar parts of Eurasia and outlying islands, while as they diverge from the pole southward they tend to split up into many species; in other words, Boreal species are more stable and persistent than those inhabiting warmer countries. The explanation of this fact is obvious. The identity of climate and environment throughout the Arctic Zone tends to preserve identity of specific characters, giving rise to a homogeneous fauna and flora, while the diversity of physical conditions and climatic influences prevailing in an increasing degree at greater distances from the pole exerts a powerful influence upon the various forms of life, producing first local geographic races or subspecies, then species, and finally groups of species constituting well-marked subgenera and even genera, giving rise to greatly diversified faunas and floras. Thus among mammals the polar or ice bear (*Thalarctos maritimus*) has no very near relative, and is replaced in the tundras by the brown and barren-ground bears (*Ursus arctos* and *richardsoni*), which run into several more or less distinct forms, as the snow bear (*U. isabellinus*), Syrian bear (*U. syriacus*), and hairy-eared bear (*U. piscator*). Besides these are the grizzly (*U. horribilis*, of which two forms may be recognized) and the black bears of America and Eurasia (*U. americanus, torquatus,* and *japonicus*); and still further southward the group becomes differentiated into several well-marked genera.

In like manner the Arctic fox is replaced to the southward, first, by the red foxes of America and Eurasia, of which several subspecies are known; second, by a number of quite distinct species, and third, by additional types, at least one of which in our own country is entitled to generic rank (*Urocyon*).

The ermine and polar hare are the sole Arctic representatives of groups which in the temperate parts of Europe and America comprise many distinct species, and in the case of the former, several well marked subgenera.

The Arctic lemmings (genera *Myodes* and *Cuniculus*) are numerously represented in the north temperate parts of the world by the genera *Ellobius*, *Synaptomys*, *Phenacomys*, *Erotomys*, *Fiber*, and *Arvicola*.

It is not to be inferred from the above remarks that the polar representatives of these various groups are to be looked upon as the parent stocks from which the other members sprang. Usually the reverse is the case, for groups of Boreal origin that now attain their maximum development in north-temperate regions have their numbers reduced in the Arctic circle to a single representative. But, regardless of centers of origin, it is here intended to emphasize the fact that types inhabiting the Arctic Zone are few in number and uniform in character throughout their distribution, while to the southward the same types become more and more diversified and new types appear as the distance from the Pole increases,* so that it may be formulated as a general proposition that in continental areas *the further from the Poles the larger the number of families, genera, and species.* †

---

*The elder Agassiz long since pointed out that "the vegetation of the two continents becomes more and more homogeneous the more we advance northward" (Lake Superior, 1850, 153). Stated conversely, this is in complete accord with the "Law of differentiation from the north southward" formulated by Allen as "a constant and accelerated divergence in the characters of the animals and plants of successive regions of the continent." (Bull. Mus. Comp. Zool. II, 1871, 379.) In a later contribution the same author speaks of the "high rate of differentiation favored by tropical conditions of climate," and adds that Arctic and cold-temperate climates are characterized by only slightly or moderately diversified faunas; that a moderate increase of temperature results in the addition of many new types; and that "a high increase in temperature, giving tropical conditions of climate," is accompanied by "a rapid multiplication of new forms and a maximum of differentiation."

† This is a general proposition intended to apply to terrestrial forms of life *collectively*, and does not conflict with the law that the maximum number of species in each particular group is found in the zone or area which is the center of its distribution.

Origin of Types and Faunas—Geologic Evidence.

In speaking of the Boreal and Sonoran origin of species and groups in the present paper, the term ' *origin* ' is used exclusively in a sense intended to indicate *present centers of distribution*— not real or ancient centers of origin—for it must be borne in mind that the history of the inhabitants of the earth is not only a history of the successive appearance and disappearance of types now extinct, but a history of great movements—of vast migrations to and fro over the surface of the globe—and little is known of the real points of origin of our Boreal and Tropical faunas and floras. The geologic evidence demonstrates that in the past large land areas have been many times joined together and many times rent asunder. The establishment of land continuity between areas previously disconnected has made it possible for new forms of animals and plants to obtain a footing and spread over regions previously uninhabited by them—often, doubtless, at the expense of the indigenous fauna and flora. Even great continents, as North and South America, have been more than once united and separated; and the last union of these continents it so recent we can distinctly trace at the present day the course and distribution of the intrusive forms.

On the other hand, in comparatively recent times, multitudes of species and genera, and even families and higher groups, have suddenly disappeared from large areas where they were formerly abundant, and some of them from the face of the earth, so that the fauna of the recent past compared with that of today presents some strange contrasts. North America in Pleistocene times was inhabited by associations of mammals not now living on this continent but found in as far distant parts of the earth as Asia and South America; for horses, camels, and elephants then lived here with llamas, tapirs, and capybaras. With them were others now altogether extinct, as huge tigers, wolves, cave bears, the great Mastodon, the Megatherium, Megalonyx, Mylodon, and other gigantic sloths.

Glacial Epoch.

The cause of this sudden extermination of dominant types is believed to have been the Glacial epoch, which is known to have driven species of animals and plants from the poles to the tropics, and which explains several of the otherwise inexplicable problems presented in the study of the past and present distribution of life.

The snows at the beginning of the Glacial epoch fell upon a continent of great forests—forests that gave shelter to multitudes of mammals and birds and other forms of life, a large proportion of which no longer inhabit America, and many of which do not exist in any part of the globe.

During the period of maximum development the great glacier is believed to have been not less than 8,000 feet in thickness in northern New England, and its southern border crossed New Jersey and Pennsylvania, and thence, curving irregularly southwesterly to southern Illinois and then northwesterly, finally reached the Pacific Ocean in British Columbia. The disastrous effect upon animals and plants of this tremendous body of ice must have reached far south of its actual borders.

The Glacial epoch is believed to have been made up of at least two principal and a number of minor advances and retreats, separated by long intervals and accompanied doubtless by corresponding fluctuations in the northern boundaries of the faunal and floral areas immediately to the south ; for it is reasonable to suppose that throughout the period covered by the movements of the ice mantle, and probably in later preglacial times as well, the forms now known as Boreal and Arctic (or their immediate ancestors) inhabited areas characterized by temperatures not very different from those they now require, and that the northern limit of each species kept at a certain uniform distance from the ice line. " Plants," says Dr. Gray, " are the thermometers of the ages, by which climatic extremes and climates in general are best measured."

Important evidence of the correctness of this hypothesis is afforded by the well known presence of colonies or assemblages of arctic species on isolated mountain summits in southern latitudes, where the altitude carries them into the low temperature of their homes in the far North. It is obvious that such colonies could not have reached their present positions during existing climatic conditions. But during the return movement of animal and plant life following the retreat of cold at the close of the Glacial epoch, many Boreal species were stranded on mountains, where, by climbing upward as the temperature increased, they were enabled to survive, finding a final resting place with a climate sufficiently cool for their needs, and here they have existed to the present day.*

Throughout the growth of the great ice mass and its extension from the north southward it is clear that the animals and plants that could not keep pace with its advance must have perished, while the steady pushing toward the tropics of those that were able to escape to the rapidly narrowing land in that direction must have resulted in an overcrowding of the space available for their needs and a corresponding increase in the severity of the struggle for existence. The sustaining capacity of a region is limited; hence such a thing as overcrowding, in the sense of greatly increasing the number of organisms a region can support, is an impossibility, for beyond a certain limit all excess of life must perish—overcrowding inevitably leading to death. The mortality in any one year may not have been great, but during the untold ages covered by the movements of the continental ice the aggregate destruction of life must have been stupendous.

Immediately upon the close of the Glacial epoch life began to reclaim the regions from which it had been so long shut out. This overflow released the tension under which the animals and plants had been struggling for ages and rendered the contest for existence less severe. Overproduction had at last found an outlet, and life became possible to a constantly increasing number of individuals. Normal reproduction was sufficiently rapid to supply occupants for the regions made habitable by the slow recession of the ice, and the advance of both plants and animals kept pace, doubtless, with its progressive increase. But the species that survived to return were only in part those driven out. Many had been overtaken by the cold or had perished in the journey southward; others were driven into inhospitable regions where the environment was not suited to their needs; others still succumbed in the struggle resulting from overcrowding, and some that outlived the first great period of glaciation perished during the second. Gilbert tells us that a detailed study of the ancient lake beds of the

* In a former communication attention was called to the circumstance that the presence or absence of such arctic-alpine colonies on high volcanic mountains may be of use to the geologist as affording evidence of the age of the volcanic activity resulting in the upheaval of the mountain, the absence of Arctic or Boreal forms indicating postglacial origin. (N. Am. Fauna, No. 3, September, 1890, p. 21.)

Great Basin "shows two lacustral epochs corresponding to two glacial epochs, and correlates the mammalian fauna with the later half of the later Glacial epoch. Presumptively this date falls very late in ·the Pleistocene period." (Lake Bonneville, by G. K. Gilbert, 1890, 397.) The mammalian fauna referred to comprises an elephant, an otter, two horses, three llamas, a deer of the genus *Cervus*, an ox, a gigantic sloth, together with three species now living, namely, the coyote, beaver, and pocket gopher (*Thomomys*). No new types came in to take the place of those exterminated; hence we in the United States now live in a region deprived of many of the groups to which it gave birth, and we are forced to visit remote parts of the earth to see animals and plants that once attained their maximum development in North America, while others that formerly flourished here are entirely extinct.

Not only are the pre-Pleistocene animals and plants now represented imperfectly and in greatly reduced numbers, but the areas at present inhabited by their descendants, except in the case of the Boreal forms, are insignificant in comparison with their former extent. It should be remembered that the refrigeration of the Glacial epoch has only in part disappeared. In early Pliocene times characteristic representatives of subtropical faunas and floras existed northward over much of the United States and Canada, and in still earlier times reached the Arctic Circle.[*] During the advance of cold in the Glacial epoch these forms were either exterminated or driven southward into the narrow tropical parts of Mexico and Central America. The retreat of cold at the termination of this period was not complete, and our continent has never regained its former warmth. Hence the expelled species were not permitted to advance more than a short distance into the region formerly occupied by them, and the tropical species have been held back and at the present day are not found except along the extreme southern confines of our territory. For example, peccaries in early Pleistocene times ranged northward over a large part of western America, while at present they are restricted to parts of Texas and Louisiana below the Red River of the South; and the capybaras, tapirs, and other tropical

---

[*] Among trees fossil remains of magnolia, sassafras, and liquidamber have been found in Greenland.

forms whose fossil remains have been found in many parts of the United States have not been able to return. The same is true of plants, for the palms, tree-ferns, and numerous other tropical types that formerly ranged over much of our country are now either altogether extinct or exist only in the tropics.

The llama and many plants now inhabiting the Andes may be looked upon as representing a class of cases in which Boreal forms were driven so far south that they actually reached the great mountain system of South America and spread southward over its elevated plateaus and declivities to the extreme end of the continent in Patagonia and Terra del Fuego. This fact has been long recognized by botanists.

The paleontologic history of the earth shows that many groups now unknown came into existence from preceding groups, gradually attained a maximum development, and as gradually passed away; but there are few records of breaks in the geologic series, or of disturbances of any kind from the earliest appearance of life to the present time, that have resulted in the destruction of so many types as the cold of the Glacial epoch. ·

CAUSES CONTROLLING DISTRIBUTION.

It is now pretty generally conceded that temperature and humidity are the chief factors governing the distribution of life, and that temperature is more potent than humidity. Illustrations of this law have been already given in contrasting the humid and arid elements of the several zones with the zone elements as limited by temperature, and it has been found in the case of mammals and birds that the effects of temperature, estimated numerically, are more than three times greater than the effects of humidity upon genera, and many times greater upon the higher groups.

Authors differ as to the exact period during which temperature exerts the greatest influence, but there can be little doubt that for both animals and plants it is *the season of reproductive activity*, and hence varies inversely with latitude and altitude. In high arctic latitudes this period is very brief, while in the humid tropics it seems to extend over nearly if not quite the whole year.*

Whether the temperature in question is the mean of a certain

* This was pointed out by the author in North Am. Fauna No. 3, September, 1890, pp. 26–27.

period or the sum of the daily temperatures for that period, or the sum in excess of a certain minimum, expressed in degrees of the thermometric scale or in calories, and how to determine the precise beginning and ending of this period for each locality, are questions respecting which difference of opinion prevails; and authors are not agreed as to whether the temperature should be taken in the sun or in the shade, or at a certain distance below the surface of the earth. At the same time it has been demonstrated by Linsser and others that a definite quantity of heat is required to complete the process of reproduction in a number of plants experimented upon—and nature's laws are not framed for isolated cases. This law is taken advantage of by expert gardeners and horticulturists who are able to so regulate the temperature of their green-houses that they can produce a perfect flower or a ripe fruit on a specified day.

A few species, particularly among plants, are so sensitive to cold that they are limited in northward range by the line of killing frost, but in the vast majority of cases the winter temperature is of no consequence. As I have already shown, "The season of reproduction for the plant, as for the animal, is the warm part of the year. After the period of reproduction the plant withers; after it flowers and fruits and matures its seed, it dies down or becomes physiologically inactive. And what the plant accomplishes in one way the animal accomplishes in another. To escape the cold of winter and its consequences, the sensitive mammal hibernates; the bird migrates to a more southern latitude; the reptile and batrachian dig holes in the mud or sand and remain in a torpid condition; the insect sleeps in its cocoon or buries itself under leaves or decomposing vegetation; and none but the hardier forms of life are left to be affected by winter temperatures." (N. Am. Fauna, No. 3, September, 1890, 26–27.)

After temperature and humidity, several subordinate though important factors remain to be considered. Among these may be mentioned the duration and actinic effects of sunlight (governed in part by percentage of cloudiness or fog and by the mechanical purity of the atmosphere). The character of the soil also determines the presence or absence of many species.*

---

*The controlling causes of distribution will not be discussed further here because they are the subject of another communication upon which the writer is engaged.

EFFECTS OF HUMIDITY CONTRASTED WITH EFFECTS OF TEMPERATURE.

With few exceptions, the Boreal zones, owing to their low temperatures, precipitate sufficient moisture to support arboreal vegetation and do not possess arid areas. The Transition and Sonoran zones on the other hand naturally fall into two important subdivisions, *arid* and *humid*, as indicated in defining their courses. As a rule the former consist of treeless plains, deserts, and barren mountains, while the latter are bountifully clothed with forests. Most of the humbler forms of vegetation are different in the two subdivisions, and differences exist also among the mammals, birds, and reptiles; but the great majority of these dissimilarities are not of the same kind as those that distinguish one zone from another. Most of them are specific—not generic—and the number of distinctive groups of high order is very much less. This may be made clear by selecting the distinctive elements of the arid Sonoran (which has the largest number of peculiar forms) in comparison with those of the humid Sonoran (or Austroriparian) and contrasting them numerically with the distinctive elements of the Sonoran as a whole compared with those of the Boreal as a whole.* Among non-pelagic mammals, the arid Sonoran has one family (*Antilocapridæ*) and only ten genera † not known to inhabit the humid Sonoran or Austroriparian; and the latter has but one family (*Didelphidæ*) and four genera (*Didelphis, Oryzomys, Scalops,* and *Nycticejus*) not found in the arid Sonoran (and the family and one of the genera are intrusions from the Tropical region), while 13 families and 27 genera are common to both arid and humid subdivisions.‡

Among birds, the arid Sonoran has no family and only 24 genera not inhabiting the humid Sonoran, and the latter has no family and but 7 genera not found in the arid, while 12 families and 31 genera are common to the two divisions.

Contrasting the Sonoran as a whole with the Boreal as a whole, it appears that there are no less than 8 families and 41

---

* The intrusive Tropical genera are here treated as Sonoran.

† These genera are: *Antilocapra, Cynomys, Onychomys, Thomomys, Dipodomys, Perodipus, Microdipodops, Perognathus, Bassariscus,* and *Antrozous.*

‡ The newly discovered genus of *Chiroptera, Euderma,* is here omitted because only a single specimen is known and it cannot yet be satisfactorily assigned to its proper faunal position.

genera of mammals and 10 families and about 100 genera of
birds distinctive of the Sonoran, and 6 families and 30 genera
of mammals and 3 families and about 40 genera of birds distinctive of the Boreal zone. In other words, taking mammals
and birds together, the arid Sonoran has one peculiar family
and only 34 distinctive genera, and the humid Sonoran one
family and 11 genera (of which the family [*Didelphidæ*] and
several of the genera are clearly intrusions from the Tropical
region), while the Sonoran as contrasted with the Boreal has
18 distinctive families and 141 distinctive genera, and the Boreal
has 9 distinctive families and 70 distinctive genera.

Only 8 families and 8 genera of mammals are common to the
Boreal and Sonoran Regions. The common families are: *Cer-
vidæ, Muridæ, Sciuridæ, Leporidæ, Mustelidæ, Canidæ, Felidæ*, and
Soricidæ. The common genera are: *Sitomys, Sciurus, Sciuropterus,
Spermophilus, Lepus, Lutra, Canis*, and *Lynx*. Several others inhabit limited parts of both regions, but are not common to these
regions as a whole.

With the possible exception of the gray wolf, not a single
species of mammal ranges throughout the Sonoran and Boreal
Zones, though a number are common to the Upper Sonoran
and Lower Boreal (Canadian); and in the case of the wolf it is
almost certain that comparison of specimens will show the animal of the southern United States and Mexico to be perfectly
distinct from that of Arctic America. The ermine is another
species of phenomenal though less extensive range, if it is really
true that the weasel inhabiting the shores and islands of the
Polar Sea is specifically identical with that found in the more
elevated parts of the Southern States—an assumption I cannot
for a moment entertain.

In the case of land birds, 18 genera are common to the Boreal
and Sonoran Regions. The number of common families is rela-
tively large as would be expected from the wide dispersal of most
families of birds. For instance, the *Turdidæ* or thrushes inhabit
North and South America, Eurasia, Africa, India, and Australia;
the *Paridæ* or titmice inhabit North and South America, Eurasia,
Africa, India, Australia, and New Zealand; the *Cinclidæ* or dip-
pers inhabit North and South America, Eurasia, India, and the
Austro-Malayan region; the *Troglodytidæ* or wrens inhabit North
and South America, Eurasia, India, Africa, and the Austro-
Malayan region; the *Corvidæ* or crows, magpies and jays, are
found in every part of the world, and so on.

Table Showing Number of Distinctive Families and Genera of Mammals and Birds of the Arid Sonoran Compared with the Humid Sonoran, and of the Sonoran as a Whole Compared with the Boreal as a Whole.

	Mammals		Birds		Total	
	Fam.	Gen.	Fam.	Gen.	Fam.	Gen.
Arid Sonoran distinguished from Humid Sonoran by..........	1	10	0	24	1	34
Humid Sonoran distinguished from Arid Sonoran by........	1	4	0	7	1	11
Common to both Arid and Humid Sonoran	13	27	12	31	25	58
Sonoran as a whole distinguished from Boreal by....	8	41*	10	100	18	141
Boreal as a whole distinguished from Sonoran by............	6	30†	3	40	9	70
Common to Boreal and Sonoran.	8	8		18		26

Descending to species, the contrast is even more marked.

The above table shows, so far as the genera of mammals and birds are concerned, that the difference between the humid 'Atlantic' or 'Eastern Province' on the one hand and the arid Great Plains and Great Basin on the other is less than one-fourth as great as the difference between the Sonoran and Boreal Regions.

These facts, it seems to me, should suffice to establish beyond dispute the subordinate part played by humidity in comparision to temperature, and should dispel any lingering doubts that may still haunt the minds of conservative naturalists respecting the necessity of abandoning the long accepted division of the United States into Atlantic, Central, and Pacific provinces.

Remarks respecting some of Wallace's Fallacies.

Wallace, in his great work on Geographic Distribution, and in subsequent writings on the same subject, greatly underrates the importance of temperature as a factor in determining the distri-

---

* *Sitomys* and *Lynx* are omitted because they range over most of the forested part of the Boreal Region.

† *Putorius* is omitted because it ranges over much of the Sonoran Regoin.

bution of life. He lays great stress upon the dissimilarity of the
faunas and floras of parts of Africa, South America, and Australia lying in the same latitude and calls particular attention to
the circumstance that although the climate may be identical
over these widely separated areas, the species and higher groups
are totally distinct, because the regions have been disconnected
since early geologic times—as if these facts were not self-evident.
On the other hand, in single continental areas where there is no
break or barrier of any kind between widely different faunal
zones, he tries to invent some unnatural reason for the differences
observed and is reluctant to admit that even in these cases
climate or climatic conditions can constitute the barriers to dispersion that undoubtedly exist. He says of climate: ".Probably
its action is indirect, and is determined by its influence on vegetation, and by bringing diverse groups into competition."

In another place he states: "Hot countries usually differ
widely from cold ones in all their organic forms; but the difference is by no means constant, nor does it bear any proportion to
difference of temperature. Between frigid Canada and subtropical Florida there are less marked differences in the animal
productions than between Florida and Cuba or Yucatan, so
much more alike in climate and so much nearer together." He
states further: "The eastern United States possess very peculiar
and interesting plants and animals, the vegetation becoming
more luxuriant as we go south but not altering in essential
character; so that when we reach the southern extremity of
Florida we still find ourselves in the midst of oaks, sumacs,
magnolias, vines, and other characteristic forms of the temperate
flora; while the birds, insects, and land-shells are almost identical with those found further north. But if we now cross over
the narrow strait, about fifty miles wide, which separates Florida
from the Bahama Islands, we find ourselves in a totally different
country, surrounded by a vegetation which is essentially tropical
and generally identical with that of Cuba. The change is most
striking, because there is no difference of climate, of soil, or
apparently of position, to account for it." (Island Life, 1880,
p. 5.)

Let us examine this statement with some care to see if the facts
warrant the assertions and conclusions of the author. But first
let me protest against Wallace's habit of contrasting insular
faunas with those of continuous land areas, in his efforts to mini-
mize the effects of climate. In most cases the great majority of

forms peculiar to an island have no means of reaching the nearest
continuous land, but in the present instance, as will be shown
later, the proximity of Cuba and the Bahamas to Florida, favored
by the direction of the Gulf Stream and the prevalence of hurricanes blowing from the Antilles to the Peninsula, have enabled
a multitude of West Indian plants, insects, birds, and even landshells to reach southern Florida, though the breadth of the strait
is an effective bar to the passage of terrestrial mammals and
reptiles.

Wallace boldly tells us, without attempt at qualification, that
" between frigid Canada and sub-tropical Florida there are less
marked differences in the animal productions than between
Florida and Cuba." Frigid Canada, in eastern North America,
is the home of the Eskimo, polar bear, musk oxen, reindeer,
lemmings, marmots, beavers, muskrats, porcupines, wolverines,
sables, shrews, star-nosed moles, and several other mammals,
comprising in all 20 genera, not one of which occurs in southern
Florida.* Florida, on the other hand, is inhabited by opossums,
harvest mice, rice-field mice, cotton rats, wood rats, pocket gophers, gray foxes, spotted skunks, big-eared bats, and other forms,
representing 13 genera and 5 families of mammals that do not
occur in frigid Canada†. In the case of birds, eastern Canada
has 26 genera that do not reach Florida, among which may be
mentioned ptarmigans, grouse, rough-legged hawks, golden
eagles, great gray owls, snowy owls, Acadian owls, hawk owls,
three-toed woodpeckers, Canada jays, pine bullfinches, crossbills, linnets, snow buntings, titlarks, winter wrens, kinglets,
and stone chats, ‡ while Florida has at least 37 genera that do

---

* The following 20 genera of mammals inhabit eastern Canada, but none
of them reach southern Florida: *Rangifer, Alce, Ovibos, Tamias, Spermophilus, Arctomys, Castor, Fiber, Arvicola, Evotomys, Phenacomys, Myodes,
Cuniculus, Zapus, Erethizon, Thalarctos, Gulo, Mustela, Condylura, Scapanus,
Sorex.*

† The following 13 genera of mammals inhabit Florida, but none of
them reach " frigid Canada : " *Didelphis, Reithrodontomys, Oryzomys, Sigmodon, Neotoma, Geomys, Urocyon, Procyon, Spilogale, Corynorhinus, Nycticejus, Nyctinomus, Otopterus.* The 5 families are: *Didelphidæ, Geomyidæ,
Procyonidæ, Emballonuridæ, Phyllostomatidæ.*

‡ The following 26 genera of birds breed in eastern Canada, but none
of them in Florida: *Dendragapus, Bonasa, Lagopus, Archibuteo, Aquila,
Scotiaptex, Nyctala, Nyctea, Surnia, Picoides, Sphyrapicus, Perisoreus, Dolichonyx, Pinicola, Loxia, Acanthis, Plectrophenax, Calcarius, Zonotrichia,
Junco, Passerella, Anthus, Anorthura, Certhia, Regulus, Saxicola.*

not reach Canada, among which are quails, turkeys, doves of several genera, vultures, caracaras, kites, barn and burrowing owls, parrots, anis, ivory-billed woodpeckers, chuck-wills-widows, cardinals, blue grosbeaks, yellow-breasted chats, mocking birds, and others.*

Thirty out of the above 37 genera breed also in the West Indies.

No less than nine Tropical American genera of birds inhabit the subtropical belt of Florida, namely, *Zenaida, Geotrygon, Starnœnas, Rostrhamus, Polyborus, Crotophaga, Euetheia, Callichelidon,* and *Cœreba.* The following Antillean species and subspecies occur in the same area and are not known from any point further north: *Colinus virginianus cubanensis, Columba leucocephala, Zenaida zenaida, Geotrygon martinica, Starnœnas cyanocephala, Rostrhamus sociabilis, Falco dominicensis, Speotyto cunicularia floridana, Polyborus cheriway, Crotophaga ani, Coccyzus minor maynardi, Agelaius phœniceus bryanti, Euetheia bicolor, Euetheia canora, Progne cryptoleuca, Petrochelidon flava, Callichelidon cyanoviridis, Vireo altiloquus barbatulus, Cœreba bahamensis.* In addition to these species, the following are restricted, so far as known, to southern Florida : *Meleagris gallopavo osceola, Chordeiles virginianus chapmani, Cyanocitta cristata florincola, Ammodramus nigrescens, Vireo noveboracensis maynardi, Geothlypis trichas ignota, Thryothorus ludovicianus miamensis, Cistothorus marianæ, Sitta carolinensis atkinsi.*

That there are corresponding differences among insects is evident from an important paper by Mr. E. A. Schwarz on the Insect Fauna of Semitropical Florida. Mr. Schwarz states: " I have come to the conclusion that it [the semitropical fauna of Florida] is entirely of West Indian origin, and that the region I shall hereafter circumscribe as Semitropical Florida does not contain any endemic forms. In other words, the distinctive fauna of southern Florida is a permanent colony of West Indian forms, much more numerous in species than it has

---

* The following 37 genera of birds breed in Florida, but none of them range north to "frigid Canada," though 30 out of the 37 are known to breed in the West Indies: *Colinus, Meleagris, Columba, Zenaidura, Zenaida, Columbigallina, Geotrygon, Starnœnas, Cathartes, Catharista, Elanoides, Elanus, Ictinia, Rostrhamus, Polyborus, Strix, Speotyto, Conurus, Crotophaga, Campephilus, Antrostomus, Aphelocoma, Icterus, Peucæa, Pipilo, Cardinalis, Guiraca, Euetheia, Certhiola, Protonotaria, Helinaia, Helmitherus, Icteria, Mimus, Harporhynchus, Thryothorus, Polioptila.*

hitherto been supposed, the number in *Coleoptera* alone
amounting, according to a very low estimate based upon my
collection, to at least 300 species not yet in our catalogues."
(Entomologica Americana, IV, No. 9, 1888.) Since the above
was published, Mr. Schwarz has had the kindness to inform me
that this semitropical insect fauna of southern Florida comprises in all not less than 1,000 species of West Indian or
Antillean insects (of which about half are *Coleoptera*), and 50
genera of *Coleoptera* and *Heteroptera* alone;* hence the total
number of genera must be very considerable.

Among the Mollusca, Dr. Wm. H. Dall informs me that 20
species or specific types of Antillean land shells are known to
inhabit southern Florida, representing 13 genera or subgenera
not found further north.†

So far as vegetation is concerned, the case is even stronger,
there being upwards of 350 genera of plants in Florida that do
not inhabit Canada ; and Professor Charles S. Sargent, in speaking of the trees of southern Florida, states : " A group of arbores-
cent species of West Indian origin occupies the narrow strip of
coast and islands of southern Florida. * * * This semitropical forest belt reaches Cape Malabar on the east coast and the
shores of Tampa Bay on the west coast. * * * The species
of which it is composed here reach the extreme northern limit
of their distribution; they are generally small, stunted, and of
comparatively little value. Certain species, however, attain re-

---

*Mr. Schwarz has kindly given me the following list of families
of Central American Coleoptera, indicating the number of genera in each
family known to inhabit Semitropical Florida, but not found elsewhere
in North America: *Carabidæ*, 2 genera; *Phalacridæ*, 1; *Coccinellidæ*, 1;
Cucujidæ, 1; *Mycetophagidæ*, 1; *Elateridæ*, 1; *Scarabæidæ*, 2; *Cerambycidæ*, 5;
Chrysomelidæ, 4; *Tenebrionidæ*, 3; *Monommidæ*, 1; *Otiorhynchidæ*, 1; *Cur-
culionidæ*, 6; *Brenthidæ*, 1 [this is the only genus which reappears at Cape
San Lucas]; *Calandridæ*, 3; *Scolytidæ*, 3; *Authribidæ*, 2. He informs me
also that 11 genera of Tropical American Heteroptera have been found in
the same belt.

†The forms here referred to are: *Strobila hubbardii* Brown; *Helix cæca*
Helix varians Mke.; *Bulimulus multilineatus* Say; *Bulimulus dormani* W. G.
B.; *Orthalicus undatus* Brug; *Liguus fasciatus* Müller; *Liguus fasciatus* var.
Stenogyra gracillima Pfr.; *Stenogyra subula* Pfr.; *Macroceramus gossei* Pfr.;
Macroceramus pontificus Gld. (also occurs in Texas); *Strophia incana* Binn.;
Auricula pellucens Mke.; *Tralia minuscula* Dall; *Melampus (Detracia) bul-
loides* Mont.; *Pedipes mirabilis* Muhlf.; *Pedipes elongatus* Dall; *Planorbis
tumidus* Pfr.; *Sphærium cubense* Morelet.

spectable proportions: the mahogany, the mastic, the royal
palm, the mangrove, the sea-grape, the Jamaica dogwood, the
manchineel, and other species here become considerable and
important trees." (Forests of North America, 10th Census, 1884,
p. 6.)

From what has been said it appears not only that Wallace's
statement that " between frigid Canada and subtropical Florida
there are less marked differences in the animal productions than
between Florida and Cuba " is wholly incorrect, but that there
exists in Florida a well marked subtropical fauna and flora consisting in the main (except in the case of terrestrial mammals
and reptiles which could not reach it) of genera, and largely of
species, identical with those of Cuba. This being the case, is it
not fair to turn the tables and ask Wallace what constitutes the
barrier that so effectually holds back hundreds of genera and a
multitude of species of Antillean or Tropical American plants,
insects, land mollusks, and birds now inhabiting subtropical
Florida? The deep arm of ocean between Florida and Cuba or
the Bahamas has proved ineffectual in checking their dispersion.
What is the more potent barrier that prevents their northward
spread along the continuous land of the peninsula ? The answer
is summed up in the single word *climate*. The temperature of
the period of growth and reproduction in the northern parts of
Cuba and the Bahamas is the same as in subtropical Florida,
but to the northward it falls off rapidly.

Respecting Wallace's statement that the difference between
the faunas and floras of hot and cold countries " is by no means
constant," and does not bear " any proportion to difference of
temperature," it need only be said that no phenomenon of nature
is more constant, and that the differences observed depend directly upon temperature. President D. S. Jordan has said : " In
many groups anatomical characters are not more profound or
of longer standing than are the adaptations to heat and cold."
(Popular Science Monthly, XXXVII, Aug., 1890, p. 506.)

That " life is distributed in circumpolar zones, which conform
with the climatic zones, though not always with the parallels of
the geographer " is a law recognized by Humboldt, Wagner,
Agassiz, Dana, De Candolle, Allen, and nearly all writers on distribution except Wallace. This law does not imply that the
same species, genera, or higher groups recur under the same

degree of heat in disconnected land areas—a manifest impossibility—but that well markèd zones of animal and plant life are
encountered in all parts of the earth in passing from the poles
to the tropics; that they owe their existence to constant differences of temperature, and that in continuous land areas each
zone may be traced completely across such areas [from ocean to
ocean in those of continental magnitude], following the windings
of the belts of equal temperature during the period of reproductive activity.

Wallace speaks thus of this law as formulated by Allen : " The
author [J. A. Allen] continually refers to the ' *law of the distribution of life in circumpolar zones,*' as if it were one generally accepted
and that admits of no dispute. But this supposed ' law ' only
applies to the smallest detail of distribution—to the range and
increasing or decreasing numbers of *species* as we pass from north
to south, or the reverse; while it has little bearing on the great
features of zoological geography—the limitations of groups of
genera and *families* to certain areas." (Geog. Dist. of Animals,
vol. I, 1876, p. 67). Mr. Allen has already pointed out the weak-
ness of this criticism (Bull. U. S. Geol. and Geog. Survey Terr.,
vol. IV, No. 2, May, 1878, 326), and I would like to add a word
respecting the extraordinary statement that circumpolar distribution affects *species* only, having " little bearing " on the " limitations of groups of genera and families." In refutation of this
fallacy it is hardly necessary to do more than call attention to
the circumstance that the transcontinental Sonoran region of
North America is distinguished from the Boreal by the possession of 7 families and 34 genera of mammals alone,* and the
North American Tropical from the Sonoran by 10 families and
upwards of 50 genera ; while the American Boreal differs from
the Eurasian Boreal by the possession of but a single family and
only 8 genera.

---

*These genera are : *Didelphis, Dicotyles, Cariacus, Antilocapra, Cynomys,
Reithrodontomys, Onychomys, Oryzomys, Sigmodon, Neotoma, Geomys, Thomomys, Dipodomys, Perodipus, Microdipodops, Perognathus, Heteromys, Felis,
Urocyon, Procyon, Bassariscus, Taxidea, Conepatus, Mephitis, Spilogale, No-
tiosorex, Scalops, Corynorhinus, Euderma, Antrozous, Nycticejus, Molossus,
Nyctinomus,* and *Otopterus.* Five of these genera have each a species
reaching a short distance into the southern edge of the Boreal Region,
namely, *Cariacus, Neotoma, Felis, Procyon,* and *Mephitis.*

MOUNTAINS AS BARRIERS TO DISPERSION.

Wallace makes the surprising statement that on the two sides of the Rocky Mountains in America " almost all the mammalia, birds, and insects are of distinct species "*—a statement that is wholly untrue, as has been long known to American naturalists. In another place he makes the general statement that mountains, " when rising to a great height in unbroken ranges, form an impassable barrier to many groups." No instance of this kind is known in North America. Even in the High Sierra in California nearly all of the families, genera, and species occur on the east slope as well as on the west, notwithstanding the great altitude this lofty range maintains for a considerable distance.† The explanation of the similarity or identity of the species on the two sides of all our mountain systems is that similar or identical climatic zones occur on both sides, between which avenues of communication exist or have existed by means of passes, either through the ranges themselves or at one end or the other. In their continuity, however, lofty mountain ranges do act as barriers to the spread of species from lower levels, but they do so *indirectly* by their effects upon climate—by interposing an arctic zone in which the species of lower latitudes cannot live. On the other hand, this same arctic-alpine climate enables many polar species to thrive in regions two or three thousand miles south of their normal continental homes.

The great Himalaya has little or no influence in bringing about the really enormous differences that exist between the faunas and floras of the plains on its two sides, for these dissimilarities are due primarily to the great difference of temperature resulting from unequal base-level, the Thibetan plateau on the north being several thousand feet higher than the plain on the south.

THE SO-CALLED EASTERN, CENTRAL, AND WESTERN PROVINCES AND THE EVIDENCE ON WHICH THEY ARE BASED.

Wallace, in common with most recent writers, divides the United States into Eastern, Central or Rocky Mountain, and

---

* Geog. Dist. of Animals, I, 1876, p. 6.
† For 320 kilometers (200 miles) the Sierra Nevada Mountains maintain an elevation of 3,100 to 4,600 meters (12,000 to 15,000 feet).

Pacific or Californian 'subregions.' He admits that the Eastern division is characterized by but a single mammalian genus, namely, the star-nosed mole (*Condylura*).

In characterizing the so-called Central or Rocky Mountain subregion, he states that the prong-horned antelope, the mountain goat, the mountain sheep, and the prairie dog are peculiar to it, forgetting that the antelope ranges from the Mexican plateau northward over the Great Plains and Great Basin, and westward over much of California; that the mountain goat inhabits British Columbia and the Cascade Range as well as the Rocky Mountains; that the mountain sheep is common in the High Sierra in California and ranges northward to the Arctic Circle in Alaska; leaving the prairie dog as the only one confined to the region.

The Pacific or 'Californian subregion' he defines as "the comparatively narrow strip of country between the Sierra Nevada and the Pacific. To the north it may include Vancouver's Island and the southern part of British Columbia." Under the head of the mammalia of this area, he enumerates 8 genera as " not found in any other part of the Nearctic region," namely, *Macrotus, Antrozous, Urotrichus, Neosorex, Bassaris, Enhydra, Morunga,* and *Haploodon.* A more erroneous statement could hardly be made. Of the two pelagic genera, *Morunga* and *Enhydra* [= *Latax*], the former does not enter the region at all and the latter barely reaches it; while of the non-pelagic genera three, *Macrotus* [= *Otopterus*], *Antrozous,* and *Bassaris* [= *Bassariscus*], range over the Sonoran region from Texas and the Mexican plateau across New Mexico, Arizona, and parts of southern Nevada and California; and the subgenus *Neosorex* occurs over pretty much the whole of Boreal America from the Atlantic to the Pacific. The two remaining genera only are confined to the Californian division, namely, *Urotrichus* [= *Neurotrichus*] and *Haploodon* [= *Aplodontia*]. Both are isolated types, inhabiting the Pacific coast country from northern California to British Columbia (the latter having no near relative in any part of the world, the former closely related to genera now living in Eastern Asia).

Hence it appears, so far as the mammalia are concerned, that these three supposed primary subdivisions of North America rest upon a misconception of fact, the *Californian* division possessing two peculiar genera, and the *Eastern* and *Central* divisions but a single peculiar genus each—a quantity of difference it would be absurd to recognize as of sufficient weight to warrant the erection of zoogeographical divisions.

In a communication already referred to (North American Fauna, No. 3, September, 1890) I stated the conclusion that the commonly accepted division of the United States into Eastern, Middle, and Western Provinces had no existence in nature, and that "the whole of extratropical North America [the Nearctic region of Sclater and Wallace] consists of but two primary life regions, a *Boreal* region, which is circumpolar; and a *Sonoran* or *Mexican Table-land* region which is unique." The so-called Eastern Province is mainly of Sonoran derivation, comprising the humid divisions of the Lower Sonoran and Upper Sonoran Zones (Austroriparian and Carolinian faunas), and of the Transition or Neutral Belt commonly known among ornithologists as the Alleghanian fauna. It contains also a southward extension of the Boreal Region along the Appalachian mountain system—mainly in the form of isolated islands.

The so-called Central Region in like manner is made up of a southward extension of the Boreal Region along the Rocky Mountain plateau, enclosed between two northward prolongations of the arid Sonoran, the one occupying the Great Plains, the other the Great Basin.

The so-called Pacific or Western Province consists of a southward extension of the Boreal Region which finally bifurcates, sending a long arm south over the Cascade Range and the Sierra Nevada, and a secondary and shorter arm along the Pacific coast north of San Francisco, together with a Sonoran element which covers nearly the whole southern part of the state and reaches north in the San Joaquin and Sacramento Valleys.

PALÆARCTIC AND NEARCTIC REGIONS.

It is no part of the purpose of the present address to discuss the distribution of life outside of our own continent, but it so happens that the Boreal element in America resembles that of Eurasia so closely that in the judgment of many eminent authorities the two constitute but a single primary region—a view in which I heartily concur. This arrangement is antagonistic to that proposed by Sclater* in 1857 and adopted with slight modification by Wallace. Sclater considers the whole of extratropical North America as constituting a single region,

* Journ. Linn. Soc. (Zool.), II (for 1857), 1858, 130–145; and again, with some alterations, in Ibis, sixth series, III, 1891, 514–557.

upon which he bestowed the name *Nearctic*, in contradistinction to the corresponding part of Eurasia, which he named *Palæarctic*, believing the two to be distinct primary regions.

Wallace, the great champion of Sclater's Palæarctic and Nearctic regions, says of the former in his most recent work on geographic distribution : " Taking first the mammalia, we find this region is distinguished by its possession of the entire family of *Talpidæ* or Moles, consisting of 8 genera and 16 species, all of which are confined to it except one which is found in Northwest America, and two which extend to Assam and Formosa." (Island Life, 1880, 41.) How he could have made such an erroneous statement is hard to understand, in view of the well-known fact that three genera of moles inhabit eastern North America and two the Pacific coast region ; and it is the more strange since on another page of the same work he states that there are three peculiar genera of moles in North America.*

He states further: "Among carnivorous animals the lynxes (9 species) and the badgers (2 species) are peculiar to it [the Palæarctic region] in the old world, while in the new the lynxes are found only in the colder regions of North America " (Island Life, 1880, 41), thus implying that there are no badgers in North America, and ignoring the presence of lynxes all along the southern border of the United States from Florida and Texas to southern California. Continuing, he mentions a number of groups which, he says, " have only a few species elsewhere." Among these are the " voles, dormice, and pikas." Pikas inhabit the mountains of western Canada and range south in the Cascades and High Sierra to southern California, and in the Rocky Mountains to Colorado. They have been reported also from the high mountains of Lower California in Mexico. The group of voles or *Arvicolinæ*, exclusive of the lemmings, is represented in Boreal North America by not less than 4 genera, 5 subgenera, and nearly 50 species. It is only fair to add, however, that some of these have been described since Wallace's book was written

" The Nearctic region is so similar to the Palæarctic in position

* In his earlier work he says: "*Condylura* (1 species), the star-nosed mole, inhabits eastern North America from Nova Scotia to Pennsylvania ; *Scapanus* (2 species) ranges across from New York to San Francisco ; *Scalops* (3 species), the shrew moles, range from Mexico to the Great Lakes. * * * *Urotrichus* is a shrew-like mole which inhabits Japan, and a second species has been discovered in the mountains of British Columbia." (Geog. Dist. of Animals, II, 1876, 190.)

and climate," he admits, "and the two so closely approach each
other at Bering Strait, that we cannot wonder at there being a
certain amount of similarity between them—a similarity which
some naturalists have so far overestimated as to think that the
two regions ought to be united." After enumerating a number
of mammals common to the two he goes on to say: " We undoubtedly find a very close resemblance between the two regions,
and if this were all, we should have great difficulty in separating
them. But along with these we find another set of mammals,
not quite so conspicuous but nevertheless very important. We
have first, three peculiar genera of moles, one of which, the star-
nosed mole, is a most extraordinary creature, quite unlike anything else. Then there are three genera of the weasel family,
including the well-known skunk (*Mephitis*), all quite different
from eastern forms. Then we come to a peculiar family of car-
nivora, the raccoons, very distinct from anything in Europe or
Asia; and in the Rocky Mountains we find the prong-horned
antelope (*Antilocapra*) and the mountain goat of the trappers
(Aplocerus [=*Mazama*]), both peculiar genera. Coming to the
rodents, we find that the mice of America differ in some dental
peculiarities from those of the rest of the world, and thus form
several distinct genera; the jumping mouse (*Xapus* [= *Zapus*])
is a peculiar form of the jerboa family; and then we come to the
pouched rats (*Geomyidæ*), a very curious family consisting of
four genera and nineteen species, peculiar to North America,
though not confined to the Nearctic region. The prairie dogs
(*Cynomys*), the tree porcupine (*Erethizon*), the curious sewellel
(*Haploodon* [=*Aplodontia*]), and the opossum (*Didelphis*) complete the list of peculiar mammalia which distinguish the northern region of the new world from that of the old." (Island Life,
p. 48.)

As already shown in an earlier part of the present essay, most
of these genera and several of the families belong to the austral
or Sonoran region and have no place in the Boreal fauna—the
only one that can be compared with the fauna of northern
Eurasia. As a matter of fact, 81 genera of non-pelagic mammals
are now recognized in ' extratropical ' North America—the so-
called Nearctic Region. Of this number 41 are found in no other
part of the world.* These genera are enumerated in the follow-

---

* The intrusive genera *Didelphis, Tatusia, Dicotyles, Procyon, Nasua,* and
Molossus, which are clearly of South American origin, are not here included.

ing table, which brings out the important fact that no less than 32, or 78 percent, are of Sonoran or austral origin, while only 9, or 22 percent, are of Boreal origin. Of these 9 genera now confined to North America, *Ovibos* inhabited polar Eurasia in Pleistocene times; *Neurotrichus* is not recognized by Flower and Lydekker as more than subgenerically separable from *Urotrichus* of Japan, and *Synaptomys* is not known except from the Transition Zone of the United States and is here classed as Boreal because of its close relationship to the transcontinental Boreal genus *Myodes*. Omitting these three, Boreal North America has but 6 genera of mammals not known from Boreal Eurasia.

PECULIAR GENERA OF MAMMALS INHABITING NORTH AMERICA NORTH OF MEXICO

Of Boreal Origin

Mazama	Zapus
Ovibos	Erethizon
Aplodontia	Neurotrichus
Fiber	Condylura
Synaptomys	

Of Sonoran Origin

Cariacus	Urocyon
Antilocapra	Bassariscus
Cynomys	Taxidea
Reithrodontomys	Conepatus
Sitomys	Mephitis
Oryzomys	Spilogale
Onychomys	Notiosorex
Sigmodon	Scalops
Neotoma	Scapanus
Thomomys	Blarina
Geomys	Antrozous
Dipodomys	Nycticejus
Perodipus	Otopterus
Microdipodops	Corynorhinus
Perognathus	Euderma
Heteromys	Atalapha

On the other hand, out of the 31 Boreal genera of North American mammals the following 24 genera, or 77 percent, are common to Boreal America and Boreal Eurasia:

Cervus	Cuniculus
Rangifer	Lagomys
Alce	Vulpes
Ovis	Ursus
Bison	Thalarctos
Tamias	Latax
Arctomys	Lutreola
Castor	Putorius
Phenacomys	Mustela
Evotomys	Gulo
Arvicola	Sorex
Myodes	Urotrichus *

In addition to the foregoing genera, which are clearly of Boreal origin, the following 12 genera of more extended range are also common to the two continents:

Sciuropterus	Felis
Sciurus	Lynx
Spermophilus	Vesperugo
Lepus	Vespertilio
Canis	Plecotus†
Lutra	Nyctinomus

Most of these genera are known to be of great antiquity, their remains having been found in Miocene strata, and it is probable that the others belong to the same category, but have thus far escaped detection, owing to their very small size. All of them attain their maximum development and numbers in the Sonoran Region in America and the analogue of the Sonoran in Eurasia; but by reason of the great length of time that has elapsed since they came into existence some of their representatives have become acclimated to a wide range of climatic conditions.

Dr. John L. Le Conte, in his report on the Coleoptera of Lake Superior, said : " The entomologist cannot fail to be struck with two very remarkable characters displayed by the insect fauna of these northern regions. First, the entire absence of all those groups which are *peculiar* to the American continent [*i. e.*, Sonoran and Tropical groups]. * * * The few new genera which

---

*As stated above, Flower and Lydekker do not recognize the American animal as generically distinct from *Urotrichus*. While I agree with Dobson in according it generic rank, it is convenient, in studying the origin of groups, to bring together such closely related types. .

†The American species of *Plecotus* are separated generically by Dr. Harrison Allen under the name *Corynorhinus*, which is adopted by the writer. The more comprehensive name *Plecotus* is here used for the reason just stated under *Urotrichus*.

I have ventured to establish are not to be regarded as exceptions. They are all closely allied to European forms, and by no means members of groups exclusively American.

" Secondly, the deficiency caused by the disappearance of characteristic forms is obviated by a large increase of the members of genera feebly represented in the more temperate regions, and also by the introduction of many genera heretofore regarded as confined to the northern part of Europe and Asia. Among these latter are many species which can be distinguished from their foreign analogues only by the most careful examination. This parallelism is sometimes most exact, running not merely through the genera, but even through the respective species of which they are composed." (Lake Superior, 1850, 239–240.)

W. F. Kirby, in a paper ' On the Geographical Distribution of the Diurnal Lepidoptera as compared with that of Birds,' states : " Had I been dealing with Lepidoptera only, I would certainly have united Dr. Sclater's ' Palæarctic Region ' and ' Nearctic Region ; ' for although the species of North American Rhopalocera are seldom identical with those of northern Asia and Europe, still the genera are the same with scarcely an exception, except a few representatives of South American genera, which have no more right to be considered Nearctic species than the similar chance representatives of African forms in North Africa or Southwest Europe, or of Indian forms in Southeast Europe, have to be considered Palæarctic species." (Journ. Linnean Soc. London, Zool. 1873, 432.)

It now becomes evident that the so-called Palæarctic and Nearctic regions are the result, in each case, of confounding and combining two wholly distinct regions—the Boreal with the Sonoran in America and the Boreal with the analogue of the Sonoran in Eurasia. Eliminating these austral elements as wholly foreign to the region to which they have been so persistently attached, there remains a single great Circumpolar Boreal region characterized by a remarkably homogeneous fauna, covering the northern parts of America and Eurasia.

Cope has shown that the chief differences between Boreal America and Boreal Eurasia are found among the fishes and batrachians—animals living wholly or in part in water. Now it cannot be insisted too strongly that while the chief factor in the distribution of aquatic animals and plants is temperature, as has been long acknowledged, yet from the very nature of the case the resulting life regions must be different—the one supplementing or being the complement of the other—for water being the medium in which the species live, the bodies of water with their prolongations and extensions, as bays, rivers, and lakes, must be studied as entities, just as we study a continent with its peninsulas and outlying islands—the means of access to a given body of water being the principal factor in determining the water-area to which its aquatic life belongs. And it should be remarked that aquatic mammals, as seals and cetaceans, and aquatic birds, as ducks and gulls, conform in the main to the laws and areas of aquatic distribution and should not be taken into account in studying the distribution of terrestrial forms of life.

Gill has said with much truth: " There appears to be a total want of correlation between the inland and marine faunas, and a positive incongruity, and even contrast, between the two." (Proc. Biol. Soc. Wash., II, 1884, 32.)

PRINCIPLES ON WHICH BIO-GEOGRAPHIC REGIONS SHOULD BE ESTABLISHED.

Wallace, in writing of the principles on which Zoological regions should be formed, expresses the opinion that " convenience, intelligibility, and custom, should largely guide us." But I quite agree with America's most distinguished and philosophic writer on distribution, Dr. J. A. Allen, that in marking off the life regions and subregions of the earth, truth should not be sacrificed to convenience; and I see no reason why a homogeneous circumpolar fauna of great geographic extent should be split up into primary regions possessing comparatively few peculiar types simply because a water separation happens to exist in the present geologic period; nor is it evident why one of the resulting feeble divisions should be granted higher rank than a region of much less geographic extent comprising several times as many peculiar types. Hence the divisions here recognized, and the rank assigned them, are based as far as possible upon the relative numbers of distinctive types of mammals, birds, reptiles, and plants they contain, with due reference to the steady multiplication of species, genera, and higher groups from the poles toward the tropics. Mammals have been chiefly used as illustrations because they answer the purpose better than any other single group, and because it is clearly impossible in a brief essay of this character to enumerate such a multitude of forms as would be necessary were equal consideration accorded to each class.

www.ingramcontent.com/pod-product-compliance
Lightning Source LLC
Chambersburg PA
CBHW032032090426
42733CB00031B/731